ONE CROSS,
ONE WAY,
MANY JOURNEYS

ONE CROSS, ONE WAY, MANY JOURNEYS

Thinking Again about Conversion

David H. Greenlee

ATLANTA • LONDON • HYDERABAD

Authentic Publishing
We welcome your questions and comments.

USA   PO Box 444, 285 Lynnwood Ave, Tyrone, GA, 30290
           www.authenticbooks.com
UK   9 Holdom Avenue, Bletchley, Milton Keynes, Bucks, MK1 1QR, UK
           www.authenticmedia.co.uk
India   Logos Bhavan, Medchal Road, Jeedimetla Village, Secunderabad
           500 055, A.P.

One Cross, One Way, Many Journeys
ISBN-13: 978-1-932805-77-2
ISBN-10: 1-932805-77-X

Library of Congress Cataloging-in-Publication Data

Greenlee, David, 1957-
  One cross, one way, many journeys : thinking again about conversion / by David H. Greenlee.
    p. cm.
  Includes bibliographical references.
  ISBN-13: 978-1-932805-77-2 (pbk.)
  ISBN-10: 1-932805-77-X (pbk.)
  1. Conversion--Christianity. I. Title.

  BR110.G74 2006
  248.2'4--dc22
                            2006026848

Cover design: Paul Lewis
Editorial team: Andy Sloan, Betsy Weinrich, KJ Larson

Printed in the United States of America

With Deepest Gratitude

To my wife, Vreni, for loving me and walking with me these twenty-one years;

To my parents, J. Harold and Ruth Greenlee, who taught me the Scriptures from my earliest days;

To Leola Fraley and my other Sunday school and Vacation Bible School teachers from my early childhood, whose names I have forgotten;

To Howard O. Jones, whose sermon God used to draw me to saving faith in Jesus Christ over forty years ago;

And to Bill Morrison, whose quiet, worthy witness touched many lives.

TABLE OF CONTENTS

PREFACE

We live in a busy world. In the marketplace and too
often in Christian ministry we are driven by values
related to performance, pragmatism, efficiency, and
profit. Many of us relish the thought of a change of pace: a
day with the family, playing a favorite sport, maybe a chance
to go fishing or to read that book we have always wanted to
finish, or perhaps to just have an afternoon to do nothing. But
if we ever do get ourselves into such a refreshing situation,
too quickly the mobile phone buzzes or we just *have to* check
to see if an important e-mail has arrived.

When I joined Operation Mobilization nearly thirty years
ago, international phone calls (at least from Asia and South
America) were rare, difficult, and expensive—a far cry from
our current Internet-enabled information addiction. Since
then the pressure to be continuously connected has become
at times overwhelming and, more often, unnecessary. Such
was my recent experience in southern Africa when my trans-

lator's cell phone went off three times as we tried to present the Sunday morning sermon together.

Why do we so rarely find the time to think or to reflect on life, God's Word, and the things that are, or should be, of most importance to us? In asking this I do not refer just to the United States or Europe but also to Korea, India, Singapore, Brazil, and beyond.

I have been a frequent participant in conferences and congresses drawing together missionaries and church leaders from many countries. Most leaders make time to discuss a program, an activity, or a new effort at evangelizing and discipling the region in question. But if you try to gather a group to sit back and reflect—to consider the basis for those activities—you may, like I have in the past, find yourself sitting almost alone in the designated gathering place.

In comparison, I recently attended a week-long conference in which I was assigned to a table of six individuals of various ages and nationalities, one of four such tables in a group of about twenty-five people. I was amazingly refreshed as over the course of a week we spent long hours together looking afresh at one of the Gospels, learning again how people became followers of Jesus and, in turn, "fishers of men." And yet I will admit that if I had known in advance that such group Bible study was to be the emphasis of the week, I might not have chosen to attend.

As I write this book I am concerned that too often we enter into mission and evangelism without really thinking through our understanding of conversion. We want people to come to faith in Jesus Christ, but do we ever make an effort to think outside of the theological frameworks we (spiritually) grew up in? Do we ever at least *try* to look at the issues through someone else's cultural eyeglasses? Perhaps such reflection could lead us to new, creative modes of encounter with those who are not yet followers of Jesus Christ—without being tied down by technique and program. Perhaps it would allow us to better understand those who follow Jesus in ways different from our own, whose journey is quite distinct from ours, or who "fish for men" using a different kind of net or fishing pole than we know how to use.

This book draws on my experience, first as a missionary's son and then as a missionary myself, in South America, North America, Europe, and the Mediterranean. It is developed from my observations of the peoples of, and God's work in, dozens of countries in most corners of the globe. My hope is that this book, wherever you read it and whatever your national origin, will help you to think again about conversion, to reflect on the wonder of God's grace, and to recognize some dimensions of conversion you had not considered before. In turn, my desire is that those new insights will help to draw you closer to God, make you more understanding of others, and enable you to be more fruitful in your service.

Since my hope is that many types of people from many parts of the world will discover this book, perhaps you have not yet come to the kind of faith and experience I describe in these pages. If so, may God use these words to draw you closer to that life-changing encounter with Jesus Christ.

I take responsibility for what I have written, recognizing that I am a learner still "in process." I have tried to adequately reference those on whose ideas I am building. My father, J. Harold Greenlee; my sister, Lois Stück; and my friend, Greg

Kernaghan, assisted me in early editing and the presentation of some ideas. Finally, my thanks to Volney James, Angela Lewis, Andy Sloan, Valerie Crawford, and the rest of the team at Authentic for their assistance in making this book a reality.

1

STARTING THE JOURNEY

I know when I came to faith in Christ. I can remember the date, can tell you the time, and could take you to the spot where I repented of my sins and trusted in Jesus Christ as my Savior.

The memory is richly alive of that Sunday evening in February 1964 in a small town in the southeastern United States. I was sitting a bit down the pew from my parents and sisters in the Wilmore Methodist Church. I cannot remember anything of the message, just the knot in my stomach as I realized I had to do *something* when Billy Graham Association evangelist Howard O. Jones gave the invitation.

Somehow I got to my feet, wiggled through the crowd, and made my way close to the already-crowded altar rail. I knew what to do, and by the time my mother caught up and asked if she could pray with me, I could tell her, "It's already taken care of."

At about 8:30 p.m. on Sunday, February 16, 1964, I came to faith in Christ.

But, in fact, if I refer to my "coming to faith in Christ," I would need to take you to several places and times and introduce you to many people. I am forever grateful to Dr. Jones for his message that night—whatever he said, it got through to a six-year-old! But in a sense he was just picking the fruit of the seed long ago planted then watered by my parents, Sunday school and vacation Bible school teachers, and others.

HOW DO PEOPLE COME TO FAITH?

How did *you* come to faith? Or perhaps better, where are you on the journey of coming to and growing in faith?

Many of us remember a specific event, even if not as dramatic as Paul's experience on the Damascus road. But not everyone fits that pattern.

Richard Peace, in *Conversion in the New Testament: Paul and the Twelve*,[1] walks the reader through the disciples' three-year "coming to faith" process recorded in Mark's Gospel. They grew in understanding and belief in Jesus as teacher, prophet, Messiah, Son of Man, Son of David, and Son of God. But unlike my Sunday evening church experience, it is hard to say when the Twelve were "born again" or "accepted Christ."

Recently I spoke with Muhammad, a man whose story has parallels to the Twelve: he and they were raised to believe in one God yet had a life-changing encounter with the

Son of God. Muhammad lives in an Asian country where both Christians and Muslims are a small minority of the national population.

There is no doubt today that Muhammad is born again, firm in his faith. There is also no doubt that five years earlier he not only had no such faith but was opposed to Christ and Christianity. Attracted to a young lady (not to Jesus!), he attended a Christmas program, even though he despised the church. The words of the song "Immanuel, God with Us" snagged his heart like a fishhook. Later, a prophetic word from a foreign pastor caused him to begin turning to and seeking Jesus. Months later he came to understand more about forgiveness of sins and that Jesus is the Son of God. His change of heart came ahead of his growth in knowledge.

When was this young man born again? I don't know, and I don't think Muhammad knows either. He has come to faith, but it is hard to identify a precise point when he was "converted."

HOW WE UNDERSTAND CONVERSION MATTERS

Why does our understanding of the timing and process of conversion matter? Richard Peace points out that "how we conceive of conversion determines how we do evangelism."[2]

The pastor who spoke the prophetic word to Muhammad had, in other meetings held at that time, called people to repent and believe—now! Just as I am thankful for Howard Jones' evangelistic call back in February 1964, there are many in Muhammad's city who are eternally grateful for the direct challenge from the pastor who visited their country. They, and I, rejoice that someone called us to come to a specific point of conversion, without delay.

In dealing with Muhammad, though, the pastor was discerning enough to see that the fruit was not yet ripe and wise enough not to try to pick it while green. In many cases, at least in non-Western settings, people will "pray to receive Christ" when in fact all they are doing is being polite, honoring their guests by going along with their wishes.

Muhammad, no friend then of Christians, says he would have been turned away by such a rushed or confrontational approach. I wonder, would Peter have turned back had Jesus' first words been "Who do people say that I am?" (Mark 8:27) rather than "Come, follow me" (Mark 1:17)?

THINKING AGAIN ABOUT CONVERSION

If the cross is the center of history, conversion is the core of Christian experience. On the one hand defined simply in terms of grace and faith (Ephesians 2:8–9), conversion is also a concept drawing out cultural, social, spiritual, and political complexities. Because of these complex factors, although there is only one cross (Colossians 2:13–15) and only one way to God (John 14:6), the ways conversion is worked out—the journeys of individual followers of Christ—are many.

In the pages that follow, I invite you to think again with me about conversion. Few readers will agree with every point I make or appreciate each insight. Many will think of things I have failed to include. Some will in fact object to the very word *conversion*. I recognize that it has become a dirty word in some contexts, stained by association with colonialism, extraction of new believers from their society, culture change, and force—a word that some say should be eliminated from our missiological vocabulary. I respect these concerns, especially when they are held by people in places where "anti-conversion laws" are a serious threat and where those who follow and serve Christ are under great pressure. I myself avoid speaking of "converting someone" or "converts from another religion," expressions that, to me, *do* tend to carry those negatives nuances.

Many, though, have thought long and hard in search of a better word in the English language (and other languages) to describe this process and event of coming to faith in Christ. So far, I have not heard any single term that conveys the richness of meaning carried by the ten letters of *conversion*. Therefore, in this volume in general I echo Andrew Walls' use of the term to refer to "the most elemental feature of the word . . . the idea of turning . . . the specifically Christian understanding of the response to God's saving activity."[3]

Conversion is a journey, a long road on a narrow way. Let's get started!

2

INSIDE OUT OR HEADING HOME?

In the early days of Operation Mobilization's ministry through its ship *Doulos*, "Hans," from northern Europe, was the supervisor of "Ray," from Southeast Asia. Ray's task was to serve customers on the ship's large bookfair and make sure his shelves were stocked and in order; Hans oversaw the shift of workers to which Ray belonged.

As I recall the incident, Hans dropped in to visit the ship's director one day. "I don't think Ray can be a Christian," he eventually said. "He spends so much time talking to people that he rarely has his shelves stocked and in order."

Shortly after that, Ray came for an appointment unaware of Hans' earlier visit. "There is no way that Hans is a Christian!" he insisted to the director. "All he cares about is work and schedules, not about spending time with people."

BOUNDED-SET CHRISTIANITY

One door and only one,
   and yet its sides are two.

I'm on the inside;
   on which side are you?

As in that old Sunday school song, we often view conversion as getting inside the door, passing a barrier between being non-Christian and Christian. However, is there a more helpful way to view conversion, a model that helps us better understand what happens when we come to faith in Christ?

Borrowing from mathematics, Paul Hiebert describes this inside versus outside way of thinking as a bounded set.[1] Bounded sets are defined by their intrinsic characteristics. My wife buys apples and bananas, but hybrid "appanas" don't exist. There are exactly eleven whole numbers including and between 0 and 10; 2 and 7 are in, –2 and 43 are out.

With bounded sets it is fairly easy to determine insiders from outsiders, at least if we know the rules and definitions well enough. I can look at the colors of football players' uniforms and tell which men belong to "my" team. An immigration inspector at the airport quickly determines from a glance at the cover of my passport if I have the right to enter through the "citizens" line or if I need to go through the "foreigners" line.

As Hiebert points out, bounded-set thinking has greatly influenced the church's understanding of "being Christian."

None of us likes to admit to prejudice or judging by externals, but probably all of us fall prey to this sin from time to time. Sometimes it stems from intercultural misunderstandings. Such was the case of Hans and Ray, the unhappy co-workers on the *Doulos*. The differing boundaries that these two men used to define "Christian" were strongly influenced by their cultural values on task and people orientations, limits they fortunately were able to learn to leave behind.

How are we influenced by bounded-set values? We may look at what beverages a person drinks, what kind of clothes she wears, the music he prefers, the political parties they support, and other patterns of behavior, and then subtly pass judgment on whether or not we think they are "saved." Beyond deciding whether or not we think people are genuinely converted, how soon we think it is appropriate to baptize them, what we teach them, and how we define "church" are all influenced by an "I'm on the inside; . . . Are you?" way of looking at things.

While we profess that salvation is by grace, our evangelism and discipleship often focus on developing the right kind of behavior and reproducing the accepted thinking—that is, the teachings that set us apart from other churches. In one Southeast Asian nation I was told of the surprise created when a leading politician's wife (assumed to be of the majority, non-Christian faith) was observed to publicly pray *not* with her hands apart, cupped upward, but with her hands folded together in front of her—the *Christian* way to pray!

Even if we boldly declare that salvation is by grace alone, too many of us fall prey to trying to live out our faith by works. In William Hendricks' revealing study of people leaving the North American church, one typical former churchgoer stated, "Almost any evangelical church worth anything will teach that salvation is by grace. But after somebody accepts grace, then grace is virtually forgotten, and the Christian life becomes some combination of faith and works." Hendricks continues, "Story after story bore this out. . . . Perhaps the greatest tragedy was that a system promising forgiveness to people and freedom from guilt ended up making so many of them feel guilty. That, in turn, led to chronic legalism."[2]

Behavior *does* matter; being forgiven is not a license to sin (Romans 6:1–2). But we live godly lives and avoid certain kinds of behavior not *to make us* followers of Jesus, not to *become* saved, but *because* we are saved, *because* we are "in Christ." Grace is a "centered set" concept—a concept centered on relationship with Jesus.

Granted, Jesus himself seemed to use this sort of boundary image in describing the sheep pen (John 10:1–18). He also speaks of entering through the narrow door (Luke 13:22–30) or the narrow gate (Matthew 7:13–14). But we need to remember that the purpose of the gate was to mark the entry to the road. While the travelers in *Pilgrim's Progress* would remind us of the importance of staying within the boundaries of the path, the key point is that the path points somewhere, the journey has a destination.

CHRISTIANITY CENTERED ON JESUS

Jesus' words about the sheepfold can be seen from a different perspective. Rather than position, the emphasis is on relationship: not *where* the sheep are, but *whose* the sheep are.

Whether safe and asleep in the pen or far away and in danger on the mountain (Matthew 18:12), the sheep are *his*.

Paul Hiebert defines this kind of thinking as "centered sets." In mathematics, we might have a set of numbers, such as 5, 10, 15, 20, etc.—numbers related by being multiples of 5. "Cousins" are people who share the same grandparents. "Real Madrid fans" are scattered around the globe but related by their passion, in varying degrees, for a specific Spanish soccer club.

In a centered-set view of Christianity, relationship and direction are key. A great scholar may know volumes about Jesus but have his back turned on the cross. Young Muhammad, mentioned in the first chapter, knew very little about Jesus but had fallen in love with, had centered his life on, Immanuel— "God with us."

When were Peter and the other disciples "born again"? Was it when someone explained "the plan of salvation" to them and they "prayed the sinner's prayer"? Or was it when they left their nets and tax tables to follow the Jesus they hardly knew? Or was it later, when Peter made his "Great Confession" (Matthew 16:16)? Was it only after hearing Cleopas' Emmaus Road story, when the Old Testament Scriptures suddenly began to make sense (Luke 24:13–35)? Or did it only take place when Jesus appeared and "opened their minds so they could understand the Scriptures" (Luke 24:36–49)?

I am convinced that the key question is not *how much* we know but *who* we know. What counts is not being inside certain boundaries of knowledge and behavior, but—by faith— being pointed toward Christ.

Let's be clear: being pointed toward Jesus is not the end goal. Centered-set Christianity focuses on *turning toward*, then *movement toward*, the center. But the order of events in this Christ-centered movement may differ among those who follow him. In hearing several testimonies of people who have turned to Christ from non-Christian religions, I have been struck by the variety of sequences of such key steps as coming to believe in the existence of one God, believing that Jesus is the Son of God, recognizing the need to repent of sin, or simply falling in love with the person of Jesus Christ.

Bounded-set thinking comes easily for most of us: it fits our desire for order and our tendency to put people in boxes, including a boxed-in Christianity. Centered-set thinking may be more difficult, and, as is true of any model, it does not give us all the answers. I believe that a centered-set understanding of conversion is more biblical than the boundary approach. Both, by the way, affirm the importance of truth. We turn to a real Jesus who lived a real, historical life.

CENTERED SETS AND EVANGELISM

Church and mission organization partnerships have blossomed in recent years. One regional group I was involved in for several years grew from a handful of ministries interested in improving follow-up of radio programs and Bible correspondence courses to a diverse, fruitful network of dozens of national churches and international ministries. Most participants in such partnerships would agree that cooperation in evangelism comes easier than in forming and developing churches. Unity in evangelism, on drawing people to Christ, is not nearly as difficult to find as cooperation in church planting, where we are more likely to disagree on issues with immediate, visible differences—for example, how and who to baptize or how the gifts of the Holy Spirit are exhibited in our worship.

But even when it comes to evangelism, a bounded-set mentality can box us in.

A few years ago a colleague in North Africa rejoiced when a friend turned to Christ. Someone in another organization, though, had a different understanding. So this second person found the opportunity to pray with the North African "to receive Christ" according to *his* rules, and then made it known that he was one of "his" converts!

In a church leadership meeting, one member expressed concern about some who regularly attend worship services but had not "prayed to receive Christ." I asked whether these people *know* Christ. The questioner seemed puzzled. How could they *know* Christ if they had not prayed to receive him? As others joined in, the discussion digressed, I am afraid, into a call that "the gospel be proclaimed" every week with "an invitation to receive Christ."

The intention was good, but I question the prescribed method. (Please do not misunderstand—I rejoice when the gospel is effectively proclaimed. As a child I put my faith in Christ as I knelt near the front of a church after an evangelist's "altar call," and when appropriate I make such an appeal at the end of my preaching today.) My concern is that although we run the risk of missing someone for whom today *is* the last day, a mechanistic, every-time-we-meet, bounded-set approach to gospel "invitations" seems almost certain to push away many more (youth especially, my teenage children remind me) who tire of repetitive, ritualistic evangelistic appeals.

We also run the danger of deceiving ourselves. Whether Jerusalem tour guides or Russian prison inmates, I have heard countless stories of people, even entire prisons or schools, "praying to receive Christ"—but what really happened? Too often the fledgling foreign evangelist "led someone to Christ" who was only repeating words as a sign of politeness or, worse, to build a relationship that might lead to a visa to Europe or the United States or some other personal advantage.

I am very much in favor of "praying to receive Christ." But beyond the call to repentance and belief, I do not see the New Testament giving us a single, prescribed method for turning to Christ. For example, can we identify at what point in Acts 10 Cornelius and his household "got saved"? Some might argue it was at the point the Holy Spirit came on them (v. 44), but perhaps it was at some undefined earlier time (see v. 2) when he and his family began to devoutly fear God. The fact that it was as Peter "began to speak" (Acts 11:15) that the Holy Spirit came on them, and *not* after hearing and considering a lengthy presentation of the gospel, suggests that the message resonated with an inward preparation—if not also an inward turning—that had already taken place.

The point is, we don't know exactly when nor how Cornelius and his family and close friends first turned to Christ, when they first were set right with God. But we know that by the end of Acts 10 they had moved from being devout God-fearers to being filled with the Holy Spirit, from limited understanding of the facts of the gospel message to a more complete knowledge of God's grace.

Going back to my friends in church who have not "prayed the prayer," to be quite honest I am not sure where they stand before God. I want them to know Christ, to be in Christ, to have the assurance of eternal life. But I have far greater assurance regarding them than I do those who—at times with great fanfare and all-church rejoicing—have "prayed the prayer" but today are nowhere to be found. Even if you, I, and many others entered onto the way of life by "praying to receive Christ," the key question is not if they have crossed that particular boundary but if by faith they *are* centered on Jesus, are *in* Christ (Romans 8:1; 2 Corinthians 5:17).

Since, as Richard Peace observes, how we understand conversion affects how we do evangelism, a centered-set understanding will lead to a different style of evangelism than a bounded-set theology of conversion. This made a significant difference in one ministry setting in which I participated.

In 1986 Operation Mobilization's ship *Doulos* visited ports along the West African coast. Recently married and having worked for two years in the head office, I read with joy of the strong evangelistic emphasis—with thousands "praying to receive Christ" after evangelistic rallies and open-air preaching, many of the "converts" filling out a decision card. I trust that some of those people were sincere and are following Jesus today; but when, a few years after the ship's tour, we asked churches in the port cities how many members had come from those ship visits, we could find very few, if any.

Four years later I was responsible for the program and evangelism of OM's other ship, the *Logos II*, as we called on many of those same ports. Again we emphasized evangelism, and we often asked people to pray to receive Christ as Savior

15

and for the forgiveness of sins. But we did not write down the names or count the numbers of those who made that initial response; instead, we invited them to a series of three meetings where the gospel was explained in greater depth. At the end of the three nights, those interested were invited to a further series of Bible studies that eventually led to participation in a church.

From this tour of West Africa we later heard of ten here, fifteen or twenty there, who were faithfully continuing in a church, following Christ. What was the underlying difference in strategy?

Late in life John Wesley stressed the importance of training and connecting those who were "awakened," hesitating to preach only once in a town for fear of doing more harm then good. On a tour of Wales in 1763, he wrote in his journal:

> I was more convinced than ever that the preaching like an apostle, without joining together those that are awakened and training them up in the ways of God, is only begetting children for the murderer. How much preaching has there been for these twenty years all over Pembrokeshire! But no regular societies, no discipline, no order of connexion; and the consequence is that nine in ten of the once-awakened are now faster asleep than ever.[3]

Wesley's emphasis, and ours two centuries later, was not on getting people to cross a boundary we had defined but to come into a lasting, saving relationship with Christ, which could best be fostered in relationship with other Christians. That underlying difference in how we understood conversion *did* affect how we did evangelism, with eternal fruit a result.

A LIFE CENTERED ON CHRIST

"It is for freedom that Christ has set us free. Stand firm, then, and do not let yourselves be burdened again by a yoke of slavery" (Galatians 5:1).

It was the early days for the Christian church. Paul and Barnabas had finished their first preaching tour of what to-day we call south-central Turkey. Many had turned to faith in Christ in Lystra, Derbe, and Antioch of Pisidia, but false teachers had come in—men who apparently accepted that Gentiles could become part of the family of believers but insisted that they must fulfill the Old Testament law.

"Anathema!" was Paul's powerful reply. "Let me, let anyone be cursed rather than preach a different gospel than the one I first proclaimed to you, the gospel revealed to me and confirmed by Peter and James in Jerusalem. Salvation is not something we earn, not a result of keeping the law—but a gift."

Paul's message was so strong in its emphasis on freedom and grace that some accused him of proclaiming licentiousness. "Nonsense!" said Paul. "You, my brothers, were called to be free. But do not use your freedom to indulge the sinful nature; rather, serve one another in love" (Galatians 5:13). Later he wrote to the Christians at Rome: "What shall we say, then? Shall we go on sinning so that grace may increase? By no means! We died to sin; how can we live in it any longer?" (Romans 6:1–2).

Drawing his letter to the Galatians to a close, Paul describes a list of "acts of the sinful nature" (Galatians 5:19–21). This taxonomy of sin describes the behavior, the specific actions, of people outside God's kingdom. By comparison, he gives no list of acts that describe the behavior of Christians. Instead, the "fruit of the Spirit" (Galatians 5:22–23) consists of character qualities that underlie godly behavior.

Turning to Jesus—the initial coming to faith in Christ—is vital. Like Paul, for some it may take place in a specific, dramatic moment; for others, like Peter and Cornelius, the precise time may not be known even if such people can say with certainty that although once they did not believe, now they do. But in the ongoing process of conversion, how does Jesus remain the center, the focus, the goal? This happens when he becomes not only the center toward which we are pointed but takes over the center of our lives. As Paul wrote, "I have been crucified with Christ and I no longer live, but Christ lives in me. The life I live in the body, I live by faith in the Son of God, who loved me and gave himself for me" (Galatians 2:20).

3

CONVERSION AT THE CORE

The young missionary sat in a jail cell in North Africa. Although he wondered what would happen to him, he was not worried. As a citizen of a powerful nation, the worst the authorities would do to him was expel him from their country. His concern rested with three or four men in cells adjoining his. Citizens of this country, a land not known for respecting human rights or religious freedom, they had already been mentally and physically assaulted for their faith. What would the next step be? Would they break? Would they turn their backs on Jesus and recite the *shahada*, the Islamic creed?

The missionary agonized in prayer for them. He began to hum some gospel tunes, hoping in some way to encourage them. Soon he heard a soft sound in reply, breathy but melodious. Although no words were sung, words formed in his mind to match those of the other prisoners' melody. The missionary pursed his lips to join the impromptu chorus of whistling:

I have decided to follow Jesus;

I have decided to follow Jesus;

I have decided to follow Jesus;

No turning back, no turning back.

TRACKING THE PROCESS OF CONVERSION

Jim Engel[1] and Viggo Søgaard[2] have given us two useful models to help us evaluate where people stand in the process of conversion. Something of a thermometer scaled to indicate where a person stands with respect to knowledge of God, attitude toward the gospel, faith in Christ, and incorporation into the Christian community, the Engel Scale is often used to reflect cognitive input—how much a person knows of the gospel.[3]

Søgaard's improvement draws out a second dimension, the affective aspect of the process of conversion. Søgaard helps us see more clearly that not just a person's knowledge is important, but also his or her attitude to the message and to Jesus Christ. One may know vast amounts about Christianity but have great distaste for it and no interest in following Christ, while another may have very little knowledge but a great love for Jesus.

These scales have proved useful in evaluation and ministry planning. Søgaard, for example, helps the missionary develop an appropriate media strategy by recognizing which media are most appropriate for the various stages in the process of conversion. Both the Engel and Engel-Søgaard scales are very helpful in comparing the progress of evangelization of different groups and their receptivity to the gospel message.

THREE LEVELS OF HUMAN EVALUATION

Paul Hiebert points to three levels of assumptions that help to form a worldview.[4] The *cognitive* level refers to the evaluation of what is fact and shapes categories of logic and thinking, including what we believe to be true. At the *affective* level, humans decide what is beautiful, what they like, how they feel about things. At the *evaluative* level, moral right and wrong, as well as ultimate commitments, priorities, and allegiances, are determined.

I find helpful a comparison between the levels in Hiebert's model and the categories used by Jesus in stating the Great Commandment: "Love the Lord your God with all your heart and with all your soul and with all your mind" (Matthew 22:37). Together these point to the need for a commitment to Jesus at the deepest level of our being. They also may help us understand why the process of conversion for some is truncated or even abandoned.

OVERCOMING BARRIERS OF KNOWLEDGE AND BELIEF

In Islam, two core Christian doctrines are denied: Jesus is a prophet, but only a prophet—not the Son of God; and Jesus did not die on the cross, therefore there is no resurrection of Jesus. These concepts are deeply ingrained in a Muslim's belief system.

When a colleague showed the *Jesus* film to a Muslim friend, the friend's children began to wail as Jesus was nailed to the cross. "They're killing him, they're killing him, and he didn't do anything." Their mother entered the room at that point and calmed the children by matter-of-factly stating, "It wasn't him; it was someone who looked like him."

These two denied doctrines dovetail perfectly with Romans 10:9: "If you confess with your mouth, 'Jesus is Lord,' and believe in your heart that God raised him from the dead, you will be saved." Assurance of salvation is promised to those who affirm that which Muslims—and, in fact, most of the world—generally deny: Jesus is Lord, and God raised him from the dead.

In my research in a Muslim country, I noted the great importance of Bible correspondence courses (BCCs) in the process of conversion.[5] The suggestion of a missionary colleague with many years of experience appears to have been confirmed; that is, Muslims often need a long time to process at a cognitive level the implications of Jesus' death and resurrection and of his being the Son of God. Working through BCCs enables individuals to do this alone, without being under pressure to dispute with anyone or defend themselves and their beliefs in order to save face.

We should not be surprised if it takes a monotheistic Muslim some months or years to overcome these hurdles. How long did it take monotheistic Jewish Peter, who lived in the presence of Jesus, to adequately grasp the meaning of his "Great Confession"—even though it was revealed to him by the Father (Matthew 16:16–17)?

I do not mean here to suggest that BCCs are the only means of overcoming cognitive barriers. My point is that the gospel has content; we believe in a real and historical Jesus. Part of the process of conversion involves dealing with these cognitive elements—something we can trace on the Engel Scale.

OVERCOMING BARRIERS AT THE LEVEL OF FEELINGS

How one feels about the gospel, the affective response, also matters in the process of conversion.

In North Africa, one of the greatest barriers to coming to faith is fear—not just fear of reprisals, but fear of being different. In his study of Moroccan youth in the 1980s, Michael Suleiman demonstrated that for the students he surveyed—who by now are adults with leadership roles in their society—to be an Arabic speaker was equivalent to being a Muslim.[6] They evidently could not conceive of an Arabic-speaking Christian. In North Africa, unlike the Middle East, the flourishing churches of earlier centuries withered and eventually disappeared after the rise of Islam. The number of national believers today is very small. Doubtless these Moroccan youths would have been surprised to know that prominent Arabs such as former UN Secretary General Boutros Boutros-Ghali and Suha Arafat, wife of the former Palestinian leader, are from their nations' culturally Christian communities.

In my research, I spoke with young men who were Muslim background believers (MBBs) about their first encounter with another MBB from their own country. Not unusual for those who did not meet another national believer until after they themselves had come to faith was the comment of one young man that, until then, "I thought I was the only Christian in my country, but meeting him encouraged me greatly."

Through BCCs, radio, or perhaps a missionary, God had drawn such men to faith despite their fear of uniqueness. But that fear of standing alone against the tide was a high hurdle that slowed down their affirmative response to the gospel.

Associating Christianity with oppression, materialism, or colonialism may repel people from the gospel. But for some North Africans, hearts set on getting to Europe, their feeling toward Christianity may be enhanced by the perceived link with the West. Granted, some motivations need to be sifted. But a young Christian leader in one country told me that it was the word "free" that first attracted him to the gospel. No, not that "grace is free," but simply that he could get something, anything, from Europe for *free*! It just happened that the word "free" was boldly printed on a coupon advertising a Bible correspondence course!

As discussed in more detail later in this book, I have observed that people tend to be drawn to Christianity by elements in the Christian faith and in the nature of the sources of witness that are congruent with that individual's personal values. These values may both stem from and conflict with the individual's culture. That is to say, lowering the affective barriers, the feeling-level obstacles, will help people move forward in the process of conversion. This may not require a complicated anthropological assessment to determine a strategy of contextualized ministry. A down-to-earth application of 1 Corinthians 13 may be what is needed.

I am reminded of a story told by Dale Rhoton, cofounder of Operation Mobilization. In the 1960s he took some African students studying in Eastern Europe to the L'Abri Fellowship in Switzerland for a weekend of interaction with Francis Schaeffer. They listened and considered his probing words, but did not profess faith in Christ. However, one day they were served a hearty meal, a very close approximation to what their mothers might have served them at home. Edith Schaeffer, it turns out, had stayed up half the night studying an ethnic recipe book in order to prepare a "homemade" African meal for them. The men not only enjoyed the meal, but Mrs. Schaeffer's love in action was a link in the chain that convinced them that Christianity was worthy of serious consideration. A loving act had done what logical argument never could do.

BARRIERS TO COMMITMENT AT THE DEEPEST LEVEL

Although intentionally reducing feeling-level barriers to conversion may attract people to Christianity, faith must go deeper. Discipleship must go on even when feelings fail. Further, although we may study and learn, our commitment to God must go deeper than the things we can logically prove or scientifically demonstrate.

I have heard (but have never seen documented) that over 80 percent of converts to Christianity from Islam fail to continue on in their new faith. The precise rate of reversion is not my concern here. Each of us, from our own experience, knows far too many who have stopped advancing or completely turned back from the way of Jesus—whether American, Nepali, or Zulu; whether atheist, Buddhist, or traditional religionist.

As I have considered the process of conversion, including the ongoing steps into discipleship, I have realized that believers need more than simply to increase in *cognitive* assent—that is, what we believe to be true about God. We also need more than a growing attraction to the gospel and to Jesus, something that takes place at our *affective* level. By the power of the Holy Spirit we all need to grow into and make a profound commitment to the Lord Jesus—something that happens in the heart at our core or *evaluative* level. We need to affirm by the Spirit: *No turning back.*

Donald Smith points to the importance of communicating a new belief in order to foster deepened commitment.[7] Being involved in public witness, he found, was far more important than receiving teaching in developing a lasting commitment to Christ.

A colleague with many years of experience in Turkey told me that believers he worked with who evaluated their lives in the light of biblical commandments were those who grew spiritually. The Ten Commandments provides a checklist of moral imperatives. Those who dealt with sin in these ten areas were those most likely to persevere in the faith.

Further, although persecution is not a panacea guaranteeing perseverance, God uses testing as a tool to forge change at the evaluative level. In my study, those North African young men who had gone through persecution (as well as those who had not experienced persecution but were not afraid of it) tended to be faithful church participants. Those, however, who were fearful of potential persecution but had not passed through it tended to be less faithful. My work did not include a historical evaluation of individuals to determine which came first, the persecution or the commitment, but the evidence seemed clear that ongoing growth in discipleship in this hostile environment was related to a "come what may" commitment to Jesus.

What was going on in these believers' lives? At the core of their being, God was dealing with their deepest commitments. For some it was as they told others of their faith that God brought about this deep-level change. For others it was as they worked through a lived-out understanding of things like the nature of God, the objective reality of truth, sexual purity, the value of human life, and attitudes toward material possessions that they went through a worldview shift and, in the process, made a deep, evaluative-level commitment to God. For yet others the shift took place as persecution forced them to choose in a society that afforded little middle ground.

COMMITMENT TO GOD THAT
REORDERS THE WORLDVIEW

When we speak of God, we do so with content based on truth revealed in the Bible. Although our eternal hope is not based on passing a theology examination, what we believe matters. It matters not only in terms of the theological concepts we believe and teach but also because those concepts—those evaluative-level commitments of our worldview—so deeply impact what we do, individually and as the church.

Much of what I have written is in reference to my experience and observations while visiting Muslim countries. However, the concepts apply elsewhere. David Wells challenges the church in America to deal with a dangerous shift at the core of belief. Instead of being centered on God, the church in America has conformed to the worldview of society and has become centered on the self. This impacts not only how we look at ourselves but also how we view the church and its mission in the world. We cater to perceived needs rather than focus on God. Even popular attitudes to "spiritual warfare," Wells concludes, are nourished more by concepts of modernity than by a right concept of God.[8]

Whether baby boomers, Generation Xers, or Muslim background believers, ours must be a "Though he slay me, yet will I hope in him" (Job 13:15) commitment to God, not one that stops when he no longer seems to meet our needs or make us feel good. Godly character, not technique, must be at the core of our training. Whether in North America or North India, contextualization—not just in the realm of evangelistic proclamation, but in the full scope of intentional application of Scripture by the community of believers—must not be confused with conforming to the world.

But we must also remember grace!

Demas and King Saul had walked close to a man of God, but had they ever personally made that deep-level commitment to God? Demas, who at one time served in ministry with Paul (Colossians 4:14; Philemon 24), reverted to a love for "this world" (2 Timothy 4:10), and consequently "the love of the Father [was] not in him" (1 John 2:15). Unlike David, the object of his jealous hatred, Saul was not a man after God's own heart (1 Samuel 13:14).

By comparison, David's repentance matched the depths of his sin (Psalm 51). Mark, who turned back under unnamed pressures (Acts 13:13; 15:37–38), was once again useful to Paul and was sought by the great apostle after Demas' abandonment (2 Timothy 4:11).

The comparisons between David and Saul and between Mark and Demas are clear. At the "performance" level, all were sinners, failures. At the heart level, the level of deepest commitments, the nature of their commitment to God was radically different. Is this the kind of Christian perfection we should seek: not so much a measure of performance or how few sins I can commit, but uniqueness of commitment? Just as my heartfelt vow of unique, lifelong love for my wife helps me through those times when I fail her, so a Spirit-enabled commitment that "I will serve no other god" helps draw me back to God's steadfast grace when I fall short of his standard. It is a commitment based on my recognition, at the depth of my being, that God as revealed in the Bible is the true God.

FOSTERING THREE-DIMENSIONAL CONVERSION

It is one thing to suggest theoretically that conversion is necessary at three levels. It is another matter to put this concept into practice in our efforts to reach the unconverted.

Fostering Conversion at the Cognitive and Affective Levels

Fostering conversion at the cognitive level requires the least mention at this point. Our libraries and our experience are full of examples of the "what, when, how, and why" of increasing knowledge of God and his Word in evangelism and discipleship.

Ample sources are also available in regard to the affective or feeling dimension of conversion. Although Christian social ministry is not to be seen as merely utilitarian—a tool in evangelism—the link between demonstration of Christ's love and an increasing interest in Christ is not a recent innovation! From Jesus' own compassion for the crowds to Bishop Cyprian leading the church in caring for plague victims in third-century Carthage (in modern-day Tunisia) to countless contemporary illustrations, we know that lovingly responding to people's felt needs tends to increase their interest in the gospel. Of course, it can also spark angry attacks from those who are opposed to Jesus.

Further, when it comes to thinking through our evangelistic strategies, writers such as Søgaard and Frank Gray, with his "Gray Matrix,"[9] help us see which evangelistic tools are most helpful, and at which stages, to attract people to Christ. We must look carefully, though, for the object of attraction.

We may think that people are being drawn to Jesus, but perhaps the real attraction is the package—not the content of our message.

Fostering Conversion at the Level of Deepest Commitment

Crisis experiences help to forge deepened relationships and confirm a new identity. In my own experience I have special links with those who suffered together at the drowning of a colleague and those who escaped from the shipwrecked mission ship *Logos* in 1988. Although I learned the finer points of apologetics at Trinity Evangelical Divinity School, my character and commitment have been shaped as I waited for God to answer prayer concerning health, financial needs, or mistreatment at the hands of unjust politicians and law enforcement officers.

In each of these cases it was God, not humans, who orchestrated the events. No Christian leader had set up a training program that included death, shipwreck, or financial crisis. At times I felt very much alone, as if it were just God and me—or perhaps, in moments of discouragement and fear, *just* me. But in each of these settings a key element of my deepening commitment to God at the evaluative level was the involvement, sooner or later, of other Christians who helped me understand what God was doing.

My suggestion, then, is that conversion at the evaluative level, the level of deepest commitments, takes place in the process of testing orchestrated by the Holy Spirit. In some cases this may take place as one decides whether or not to witness, to publicly identify oneself as a follower of Christ. Even in culturally Christian countries such as Catholic Colombia, where I grew up, or the Orthodox land where I lived while writing this book, public testimony of a faith that cuts against the dominant religion is no small matter. For others the test may come in an encounter between the way we once lived and the way God now expects us to live (see Exodus 20:2–3; Joshua 24:14–15; Colossians 3:1–17).

God often uses other Christians to help us through the testing process; but, as for David waiting patiently in the slimy pit for God (Psalm 40:1–2) and Abraham accompanied only by young Isaac as he went up the mountain (Genesis 22), there may also be periods of isolation. Perhaps even worse than feeling alone is the presence of self-appointed advisors such as those who came to Job. God knows the stubbornness and treachery of our hearts; he tests us through affliction for his own sake (Isaiah 48:11). The testing of our faith develops perseverance (James 1:3), but it also sorts out those who respond initially with joy—at the affective level—but have no real root (Luke 8:13). We may not understand the testing process or the apparent absence of God, but we can be assured that "he knows the way that I take; when he has tested me, I will come forth as gold" (Job 23:10).

Testing is a normal part of Christian experience. We should take appropriate steps to alleviate the suffering of our brothers and sisters (1 John 3:17–18). But, as an Iranian Christian leader recently told me, "We want the Christian church to be safe, but safety is not the only goal. The goal is to preach the gospel at the cost of death if necessary. If our only approach is to bail out the Christian church at the cost of not leaving a witness in the area, then something is wrong."

Ajith Fernando is concerned about the inability of too many Christian leaders and missionaries to handle frustration and strain, in particular that linked to ministry among the poor. We have emphasized the joy of the Christian life while forgetting the cross. But we cannot teach others who suffer, or mentor those going through testing, unless we ourselves are vulnerable to what they experience.[10] Could it be, at least in part, that the new believers referred to in the opening story of this chapter did not recant because the shared vulnerability and faithfulness the missionary demonstrated in prison was a continuation of the pattern of discipleship they had lived out together in less demanding times?

THINKING ABOUT CONVERSION IN THREE DIMENSIONS

Adding this third evaluative dimension complicates the graphic models, easy to visualize, suggested by Engel, Søgaard, and Gray. A three-dimensional graph is clear in my mind but would likely be confusing if printed on the pages of this book. The importance of this third dimension is that it reminds us to think of an element of the conversion process that we too often overlook.

Søgaard and Gray help us think through appropriate media based on a person's or group's location on the knowledge and feelings grid. However, how does one distinguish the necessary ministry for those with the same location in these two dimensions but with radically different commitments to the gospel at the evaluative level? I think, for example, of the many *simpatizantes* (sympathizers) to the evangelical cause in Colombia as I was growing up there. They knew a fair bit about the gospel; they liked what it did in the lives of their friends or even their family; but, unlike their wives or children, these likeable men would not make that deep-level commitment to follow Jesus.

Recognizing such differences at this evaluative, commitment level will help us change our approach. Even at the risk of alienating them, for some it might be a challenging word such as Jesus gave the rich young ruler. But Jesus did not leave it at that; he also used this encounter as a chance to teach, to mentor his faithful disciples and thus deepen their commitment (Matthew 19:16–30). Bringing change in the worldview requires Spirit-enabled teaching and mentoring—a personal touch rather than a choice of media.

ABOVE ALL ELSE, GUARD YOUR HEART

The process of conversion and discipleship is lifelong. None of us follows precisely the same journey, although we will pass many of the same milestones. Individually, and collectively as the church, we must seek to be transformed by the renewing of our minds, not conformed to the world (Romans 12:2). This involves a profound commitment to God at three levels: heart, soul, and mind; evaluative, affective, and cognitive.

When times of testing come, the knowledge and feeling levels cannot be disengaged from the evaluative level. But we must be sure that we do not neglect our deepest commitments, at the heart level, both in our own lives and as we lead and disciple others. Let us not neglect the words of wise King Solomon, who failed to heed his own astute advice and made shipwreck of his spiritual life: "Above all else, guard your heart, for it is the wellspring of life" (Proverbs 4:23).[11]

4

GROUPS, FAMILIES, AND ANYONE WHO BELIEVES

John and his team had waited patiently and prayerfully for the Southeast Asian islanders of "Anotoc"[1] to come to faith in Christ. One morning John meditated on Isaiah 25:4, reflecting on the God who is a shelter from the storm and a refuge for the poor. As he considered the passage, the telephone rang. An urgent voice cried, "There was a strong windstorm that destroyed many houses in Anotoc. Some of the villagers were killed." Shortly after surveying the devastated houses, John's team agreed that Isaiah 25:4 applied to the scene of destruction. The poor villagers needed God to be their shelter and refuge.

The team, made up of expatriates and Christians from other parts of the country, responded to the need with their limited resources, working with the devastated villagers to repair sixteen houses. The national members of the team naturally shared the gospel by introducing God as the shelter and refuge.

After two months the team invited an "insider" evangelist to speak to the group, a man who kept many of the traditional ways of the people but truly followed Jesus. Welcomed by the villagers, he preached in their language for about four hours, from the Law to the Gospels. The villagers were greatly moved, and all twenty-five present raised their hands, indicating their decision to accept Jesus as their Savior.[2] In the months that followed two further clusters of villagers in a similar way corporately and publicly professed their turning to Jesus.

ONE PERSON AT A TIME?

I was deeply touched by the Sahel famines of the 1970s. I remember watching, toward the end of the decade, a World Vision media production in a meeting room at the University of Colorado.

"How do you feed a hungry world?" the announcer asked, after photos gave faces to the shocking statistics of global hunger.

"One person at a time," was the gentle reply.

This phrase has been used many times and by many people, but that presentation had an indelible impact on me. In the slide show, "one person at a time" captured the core issue of serving hungry people. It also points to the key event of Christian mission: a repentant sinner coming to saving faith in Christ.

I knew in 1979, as I do now, that feeding a hungry world or winning people to faith in Christ was not a task left to me alone. It would take 200 years for me to merely say a quick, one-second "hello" to each of the world's six billion plus inhabitants alive today, neatly lined up, with no breaks for me to rest—not even counting those who would be born during the protracted waiting period! Fortunately the world does not wait on me alone to spread the good news!

I am glad that not only is world evangelization a shared task for the whole church but that there are valid, vital ways to communicate God's love to families, groups, and communities. "One person at a time" is important, but Jesus demonstrated fruitful preaching to the masses as well as intimate, life-changing, one-on-one talks with Nicodemus and the woman at the well (John 3, 4).

So how is it that people really do come to faith? Must conversion, by definition, be "one person at a time"—an individual decision—or can it occur as the conclusion of a group?

COMING TO FAITH AS AN INDIVIDUAL EVENT

When I came to faith in Christ, I prayed by myself in response to the evangelist's call. In fact, by the time my mother caught up with me at the front of the church, I could tell her that I had already done what I needed to do!

And yet it is hard to say that mine was an entirely individual event. I had often seen people "going forward" at our church. (I remember being puzzled one night when my father, a seminary professor, "went forward," since I thought he was already a Christian. He had, of course, gone to pray with a student who had responded to the invitation.) As I went forward that February evening, the devil may have been resisting, but the social message in that Christian college and seminary town was pulling me toward the altar, confirming that I was doing the right thing.

I am aware of some who have come to faith in Christ in a far more individual way than I did, such as the Algerian who, after living out his faith alone for many years, recently came into face-to-face contact with other believers for the first time. Those encouraging this Algerian to believe were far away, connected only through radio broadcasts; most people close at hand would have vehemently opposed his newfound faith if he had dared to say anything at all about his radically changed beliefs.

Some years ago I was involved in a partnership of mission agencies seeking to develop ministry in a country known for its opposition to the gospel. We were aware, at the time, of only ten people who indicated that they had come to faith in Christ. (Even today the number we know of is small.) For those ten, their only contact with fellow believers was by radio broadcast and occasional exchanges of letters with the broadcasters in Europe. Eight of the ten were totally isolated; two of them knew each other because one had helped the other come to faith. Nine, then, came to faith through radio broadcasts without (as far as we know) face-to-face contact with Christians either before or for many years after coming to Christ.

Of course these isolated followers of Christ did not want to be alone. They had been drawn to faith in Christ, but the incredible pressures of their society and the government security services kept them from enjoying fellowship with other believers. Even a visit by a foreign Christian proved impossible to arrange.

Only God knows the number of secret believers scattered around the world, those who have trusted in Christ but are unable or unwilling to publicly make their faith known. But whether public or private, with social encouragement or not, my decision and theirs were in large part personal decisions, as were the conversions of the Roman official in Paphos, Cyprus (Acts 13:6–12) and the Ethiopian eunuch (Acts 8:26–40).

Perhaps more common in situations with strong opposition to the spread of Christianity are the quiet but not entirely secret groups of Christ's followers. In the face of strong opposition a combination of factors may draw these men and women to Christ, but this usually includes the loving witness of another Christian.

As mentioned earlier, my research in a North African setting in the mid 1990s found that young men who had been witnessed to by a foreign Christian worker were greatly encouraged when they finally met others who, like them, had turned from Islam to Christ. "I thought I was the only one!" was a common exclamation before describing the great encouragement of finding that they were *not* alone, not traitors to their society. These young men came to Christ individually but benefited from the encouragement of Christians both from abroad and from their homeland.

GROUP DECISIONS TO FOLLOW CHRIST

Not all New Testament conversion stories are of individuals. Acts 10 tells the story not just of Cornelius but also of his "relatives and close friends" (Acts 10:24). In recounting Paul's initial visit to Philippi, Acts 16 describes the conversion and baptism first of Lydia and her household and then of the jailer, who, together with his entire family, believed and was baptized the same evening. Other accounts in Acts refer to the social interaction among Paul's listeners, for example the hostile Thessalonians (17:1–9) and the noble Bereans who examined the Scriptures together (17:10–15).

At the other end of the spectrum from the isolated secret believers are the *people movements* that have taken place among nineteenth- and early twentieth-century Dalits (outcastes) of India and tribes of the region stretching from the borders of India, China, and Myanmar to northern Thailand. Even at this time a new movement is unfolding among India's Dalits, as—along with having a quest for their long-denied freedom and human rights—many thousands have turned to faith in Jesus Christ.[3]

The Motilones, a tribal people of the jungles near the Colombia-Venezuela border, experienced such a group turning to Christ as well. Bucking the advice of wiser and more experienced missionaries, nineteen-year-old Bruce Olson headed into the Colombian jungle, where—surviving a spearing—he was taken in by the Motilones, known for their violent response to the incursions of outsiders.

Over time Bruce learned the Motilone language and began to learn their ways. God worked among the Motilones, and Bruce attempted to explain to them the story of the Bible. One night "Bobby," who alone had come to faith, presented the gospel in traditional epic ballad style, singing for fourteen hours while swaying through the night in hammocks. Rather than one or two coming to faith, a large number who had heard the ballad decided to "walk on Jesus' path," a group decision that has not only given the hope of eternal life but helped the tribe respond to the growing economic and political challenges they face.[4]

CAN WE FIND A METHOD TO FOLLOW?

Although we can look at group decisions and describe what has happened, I find it difficult to move to prescription: if only we follow certain steps (and, of course, pray enough!) a group decision for Christ will result.

Some group decisions arise from methods that we almost certainly do *not* want to follow. In the year 772 Charlemagne managed to bring the rebellious Saxons into his European realm. Subjects became Christian converts, at least in name, with baptism administered as a sign of integration into the realm. Charlemagne did not stop there, though; he arranged for missionaries to be sent. As a result, in Kenneth Scott Latourette's words, "Whether by force or by quiet instruction by missionaries, the Saxons became staunch adherents of their Christian profession. In the next period they were to become bulwarks of the faith."[5]

Conversion took place, but is this a method we would want to follow today? Although World War II was not a battle for

Christian expansion (and for the moment putting some major ethical questions aside), the low response of the vanquished Japanese compared to the dramatic church growth among the liberated Koreans indicates that, even on pragmatic grounds, Charlemagne's methods are ones we can learn from but prefer not to copy!

The work of Boniface and his colleagues, in the years just before Charlemagne, provides a more positive example. It was not unusual in that time for a group to become Christian, and be baptized, under the influence of their ruler. Along with reform of the existing church, Boniface's task involved "the long and patient process of trying to make Christians in deed of those who had become Christians in name," missionary practice that Bishop Stephen Neill points to as key to the development of the "rules and practices of penitential discipline" so influential in the medieval church.[6]

Perhaps the situation Boniface faced 1300 years ago has been stood on its head in Europe today. Rather than teaching and making true disciples out of those who had recently become Christians in name, a major challenge to the church today is the discipling of those "cultural Christians" whose inherited Christianity needs to be transformed—converted—into vital faith in Christ.

While serving as European Union Commission President, Romano Prodi recognized this need. Reporting on the May 8, 2004, *Together for Europe* day, drawing together 10,000 Catholic, Anglican, Evangelical, and Lutheran Christians one week after the enlargement of the EU, columnist Austen Ivereigh referred to Prodi's speech:

The EU has four great objectives, he believes: caring for the weakest, upholding the rights of others, reconciliation, and overcoming fear. The last two in his list related to war and terrorism. . . . War, he said, fuels terrorism and therefore could not be the answer to it. The task of Christians was to counter the logic of fear and war with the antidote of faith.

As the fathers of the EU were committed Christians, unafraid to seek guidance from their faith, said Prodi, so must Christians now be the leaven of the new Europe, nurturing—together with other faiths—the soul of the European project.[7]

Would Boniface be pleased with Europe's spiritual nurture in the twenty-first century?

FOSTERING MOVEMENTS TO CHRIST

At a recent consultation, Dudley Woodberry, noted Christian expert on Islam, referred to three bottlenecks in the spread of the gospel among Muslims: the initial coming to faith of the individual, getting believers integrated into churches, then seeing individual churches turn into wider movements in society. At the same meeting, a veteran missionary looked back on changes over the past twenty-five years. Earlier, she remembered, we only spoke of scattered believers in Christ from a Muslim background; now we hear of hundreds and thousands, and of many churches made up of those who have come to faith in Christ.

We rejoice in the individuals, but we long for the masses. We thank God for a single church, shining its light into the darkness, but we long for a move such as happened in Korea in the twentieth century, where church buildings dotting the landscape symbolize the incredible spread of spiritual vitality and renewal among the people during those years.

Is there a way to foster movements, to get away from what Donald McGavran described in India as people coming to Christ against the social tide?[8]

David Garrison has researched and popularized the concept of a *church planting movement,* "a rapid multiplication of indigenous churches planting churches that sweeps through a people group or population segment."[9] While he specifically warns against a prescriptive, cookbook approach, Garrison points to ten elements present in every church planting movement he has studied and ten further features present in most movements. He lists numerous things to do, choices to make, and leadership styles to adopt in the attempt to foster a church planting movement—all, of course, under the leadership of the Holy Spirit. Of the combined twenty common elements of church planting movements, there are four passive factors: findings that do not point to things the evangelists and new churches should *do* or *be*, but rather to social issues to which they must respond. These social context characteristics of church planting movements include a climate of uncertainty in society, insulation from outsiders (especially in the sense of resources from the church), and a high cost for following Christ.[10]

More pertinent to the theme of this chapter is the fourth of those social issues: the principle that church planting movements almost always spread through webs of family relationships. In highly communal societies, those who are ready to make an *individual* decision to follow Christ may be those who are on the edge of society—not those who will naturally help draw others to Christ. In church planting movements around the world, Garrison has observed that "new believers seize the initiative, taking the gospel to their family first, even in the face of severe persecution. . . . Meeting in homes has greatly accelerated this family-based conversion pattern often leading to an entire clan's conversion to the faith."[11]

Other missiologists have researched and described *insider movements* (discussed further in chapter 6), especially involving Muslims coming to faith in Christ. These growing groups of believers, which retain many of their outward cultural and social practices, might also be termed *congruent communities* of believers. We will explore the concept of congruence in chapter 5, but here again I note the importance of *community*. Although not described in the church planting movement terminology used by Garrison, these insider movements also tend to be characterized by the spreading of faith along existing family and social networks in communitarian societies.[12]

On the other hand, a people or nation being a communitarian society, in the terminology of intercultural studies experts Charles Hampden-Turner and Fons Trompenaars, does not mean that a movement to Christ will come easily in that setting! That factor is important but not determinative. An exception among northern European nations, France is highly communitarian, lying between China and the Philippines near the top of Hampden-Turner and Trompenaars' scale of national cultural values; yet the French are far more resistant to the gospel than the Chinese or Filipinos. Likewise, the people of Egypt, the most communitarian country in the Hampden-Turner and Trompenaars study, demonstrate little turning to Christ from Islam, while Nepal, second only to Egypt on the scale, has seen amazing church growth in the past decade.[13]

ENCOURAGING ANYONE TO BELIEVE

Christ died for sinners. Individual humans must repent of their sins and believe in Jesus Christ in order to be set right with God and receive the promise of eternal life. Because God loves the whole world—all of humanity—*whoever* believes in the Son will have eternal life (John 3:16). Jesus boldly proclaimed, "If anyone is thirsty, let him come to me and drink" (John 7:37).

Thus conversion, coming to faith, is for the individual. Some people come to Christ individually, bucking the crowd, standing against the common views and values of society.

In a North African country in the 1990s, we counted about thirty men and women who had professed faith in Christ.[14] Although there were two married couples, virtually all of the rest found fellowship with one another but without the joy of believing family members. In general, they had come to faith "against the social tide" without any support from family or from friends who were also in the process of coming to faith. And then God began to change things. Many factors were involved, but a key element of growth was that suddenly brothers and sisters were coming to faith together—or leading each other to faith! Some rejoiced over the salvation of a spouse. Eventually the movement plateaued, and the numbers are still not large; but this reverse in the trend was significant, with faith being shared within the normal close kinship and friendship structures of society.

As in the description of my own "personal decision" to follow Jesus Christ, we often emphasize the individual aspect of conversion—that God's gift of eternal life is available to *anyone* who believes. On the other hand, we should recognize that social factors and groups may encourage (or discourage) people in the process of conversion, although at the risk of nominal, superficial participation when the new faith is not internalized by each individual.

We come to the same cross, but we can provide no prescriptive template that describes every situation, no roadmap that describes the route everyone must follow. Some seem to walk alone while others come in groups, or at least with some sort of shared experience. How is this kind of corporate identity found? In the next chapter I will review a famous missiological theory and offer my suggestions to improve it.

5

CONGRUENCE, CONVERSION, AND CHRISTIAN WITNESS

"You mean, you are *evangélicos*?"

The Minister of Education and his personal assistant were touring the mission ship *Doulos*. With a German friend, I had coordinated preparations for the first-time visit of the ship to this Latin American country and had the privilege of hosting these dignitaries on their official visit to the vessel.

"Yes," I replied.

"I thought *evangélicos* were people like . . ." the assistant said, referring to groups in the economically challenged areas of town who were known for their nightly meetings and whose powerful loudspeakers carried the message, uninvited, into homes for blocks around.

Although citizens of different countries, in some ways my two guests from the educated elite of the country had more in common with me and others of the international crew of the ship than with the poor of their own country. Not surprisingly, they were more open to our words of witness than they would have been to the Pentecostal preacher whom they might denigrate but whom I considered a brother.

A CONTROVERSIAL PRINCIPLE

People like to become Christians without
crossing racial, linguistic, or class barriers.

Donald McGavran[1]

The Homogeneous Unit Principle, or HUP, has been the center of debate since the publication of Donald McGavran's landmark book, *The Bridges of God*, in 1955.[2] McGavran's views arose from some thirty years of missionary service with the Disciples of Christ denomination in India. Disturbed by the seeming lack of response to the majority of mission work, he was intrigued by the occasional large movements to Christ.

Close to McGavran's heart, India was a source of his evidence for the validity of the HUP. There had been some people movements, "a truly Indian way of becoming Christian,"[3] but much of the mission work had been according to the "one-by-one-against-the-social-tide pattern."[4] The result, extracting people from their society, turned new converts away from their people and cut them off from further witness to them.[5] Multiethnic congregations, said McGavran, are the most typical in India, but monoethnic congregations are the most natural there.[6]

McGavran's work was criticized, but the publication of *Our Kind of People* by his student C. Peter Wagner unleashed a storm. Wagner asked whether it is bad that eleven o'clock Sunday morning is the most segregated hour in America. His argument was not in favor of dominant racism but, on the contrary, in favor of expression of minorities and the growth of the church among them. The call for heterogeneous churches, Wagner argued, too often is worked out in practice as pushing African-Americans to act like majority whites and thus repelling them from the church.[7]

Analyzing Paul's teaching, Wagner argued that the apostle's concern was with salvation, not with crossing racial or social barriers. There are no second-class Christians, but conversion does not change social status—as Paul explicitly tells the believers to be content in their current state.[8]

Wagner admitted that his words could be distorted to substantiate the formation of a Ku Klux Klan church or a church of prostitutes, with the members not significantly changing their ethical behavior or racial views. But he said that was patently not his point. Exclusive worship and membership are wrong. But a strong sense of peoplehood is not racism. The point is to give people a choice, options that facilitate their becoming Christians.[9]

CRITICS RESPOND

"No evidence!" was the resounding cry of René Padilla to McGavran and Wagner. The only peoplehood for Christians, he said, is the peoplehood of 1 Peter 2:9: the royal priesthood and holy nation of God. The act that reconciles people to God also introduces them to the community of Christians, the church. Further, Padilla claimed, the HUP accepts uncritically too much of the world and its ways. We are to be "an embodied question mark," not a quotation of society.[10]

Other missiologists and theologians found it difficult to fully accept the HUP yet recognized some value in it. Challenging its "slender base" of Matthew 28:18–20, David Bosch discounted the validity of the HUP as an ecclesiological norm but recognized its usefulness as a communications tool.[11]

In his book, which included McGavran's final article dealing with India, Ezra Sargunan identified five key areas that must be considered in mission strategy in India. First, we must recognize that caste pervades Indian society. Second, we must recognize that the customs of India are very old and deeply engrained; they will not quickly change. Third, we must see the importance of family. Ostracism is "the greatest misery" that can befall an Indian villager. Fourth, we must see that religiosity (and caste must be seen through religious eyes) is an integral part of Indian life. Finally, we must recognize that India is conservative and very slow to change.[12]

CONGRUENCE, NOT HOMOGENEITY

*People are more likely to come to faith when
their own cultural values are significantly
congruent with the cultural values of the
witnessing Christian community and the means of
communicating the gospel.*

I suggest that this new principle, which I call the Congruence of Cultural Values (CCV) principle, gives a more adequate description of how God is at work than does the HUP.

David Britt originally stimulated my thinking on this issue when he suggested a new model that moves beyond the HUP.[13] Analyzing the growth of congregations in the US state of Kentucky, he found that *congruence*, not homogeneity, was the key social predictor of the growth of churches. His emphasis on cultural symbols opens the window for insights hidden by an emphasis on function, often the anthropological basis of popular missiology and in particular of much of the thinking about "people groups" and "church growth."

Similar to the assumptions of the HUP, Britt's observation indicated that we are attracted to people of like values. The difference between homogeneity and congruence, however, lies in the relationship between those inside the congregation and those outside. A congruent congregation has a relationship with its context. Its values parallel (even if not uncritically accepting) the values of the community in which it is found.

Congruence refers to the overall fit and the ease of transition between the old and the new, between the former faith and set of values and Christianity. It refers to a low level of barriers to conversion and church growth due to mismatches in values and meaning attached to symbols. Congruence may also indicate a match between the needs felt by outsiders and their sense that the Christian congregation can help to fulfill those needs. However, it should never mean devaluation of the cross and discipleship.

This emphasis on relationship and values, including change and conversion of values as the whole person is transformed, enables this new principle to be explored and developed in ways that do not attract the same theological criticism as was properly directed at the HUP.

CONGRUENCE WITHIN THE CONGREGATION

The international church I helped to lead for several years grows slowly, our numbers going up and down with the normal waves of expatriate comings and goings, and occasionally an individual or family professing new faith. The Iranian group linked with us has grown more rapidly. Compared to those in our congregation, the openness of these new Christians (the term they use to describe themselves) to the gospel relates somehow to the factors leading them to leave their homeland and take refugee status. Their Farsi-speaking fellowship is characterized by homogeneity of ethnic and religious origin. They enjoy the crossover of fellowship with our multinational congregation, but they obviously feel most at home without the challenges of the English language. Similar comments could be made regarding the rapidly growing churches in our city made up of guest workers from the Philippines and Sri Lanka, their mother tongues and native foods being characteristic of their worship styles and fellowship.

The HUP applies in these congregations. But the HUP, linked to ethnic homogeneity, does *not* describe our multiracial, English-language congregation with members from over fifteen nationalities! In all these cases, however, the Congruence of Cultural Values principle applies.

There is something that unites and attracts Swiss, Swedes, Ghanaians, Americans, and people from over fifteen other nations—including some Cypriots who choose to worship with us rather than in one of the handful of local Greek-language evangelical churches. We include housemaids, marine engineers, schoolteachers, military personnel, businesspeople, and, whether they use the term publicly or not, missionaries. What is it that attracts us to fellowship in *this* church? I don't think it is our middle-of-the-road evangelical doctrinal approach. I believe the attraction is rooted in the *congruence of our cultural values* common to expatriates abroad (or, in the case of most of the Cypriots in our church, the values they acquired during their years living in other countries). These common values find expression in our worship, fellowship, and teaching.

If we were transplanted to the home country of any group within the church, doubtless our sense of linkage to those in the church who are nationals of that country would change. They would almost unavoidably take on a different relationship to the rest of us, no longer sharing with us as expatriate, cultural outsiders. Even here, if our worship celebrations and fellowship take on the tone of a single dominant nationality, the interest of other nationalities decreases.

The church should be congruent with its context where it can be, such as choosing to worship with salsa and samba or with Bach oratorios. Style of expression (with all of the attendant importance of symbolism and ritual) and timing of gatherings are some of the more obvious areas in need of congruence. At the same time, we must be sensitive to deeper cultural values, issues that may be hidden beneath the surface, such as the differences in value placed on achieved social status (for example, through hard work and study) as compared to ascribed status (for example, through inheritance).[14] But the church must also lead and challenge society; we are not to be congruent with evil values. The church must maintain a prophetic stance against sin.

One must not assume that congruence only deals with Sunday morning worship together. "Church" is more than a one- to two-hour service; we are a community of redeemed people. Our entire lives as a community are the subject of this discussion. With that in mind, let us consider how *congruence* is a useful term in describing the desired emphasis and style of our communication to those around us.

CONGRUENCE AND CHRISTIAN WITNESS

Recently I watched *Training Day*, a Denzel Washington movie. It is a rough film. I found myself disturbed, not so much by the coarse language and the corruption portrayed in the film, but by the challenge of the Los Angeles gang and ghetto communities. Before going to bed, I sat on our porch under the autumn Mediterranean stars, asking God how in the world we could reach people like that and admitting my own fear and incompetence to try. I would feel far more at ease engaged in witness in an African village or Middle Eastern city than in the section of Los Angeles depicted in the film, a city in the country that is supposed to be my homeland! David Claerbaut has helped me see that although I am comfortable in many intercultural settings, my nominally middle class values are highly incongruent with the values of the American inner city.[15] If I were to minister in such a setting I would need to take intentional steps to listen and learn and develop an adequate servant-hearted approach to the people.

Missiologists have described the proper approach to a particular setting with various terms. "Contextualized ministries" and "inculturation" are frequent descriptors. "Incarnational ministry" adds more to the theme, with a suggestion of Jesus' own incarnation as a model for our ministry.

I would suggest that considering the congruence of cultural values between those in the communication cycle of witness is helpful.

An Example from Amsterdam

Along with students in an urban ministry class, I have toured two coffee shop-style outreach centers near Amsterdam's central train station. One focuses on youth from the suburbs who come into the city looking for a good, somewhat risky, evening out. The other focuses on ministry to the prostitutes of the area.

One coffee shop is painted in dark, powerful colors; the other is almost sparkling white. The first is characterized by heavy music and is hosted by staff having an outer toughness while offering (almost) free expression from the coffee shop's stage; the second has a light feeling, the workers characterized by a soft-spoken, loving gentleness. It is the first that caters to the youth whose lives have not yet been ruined by drugs and sexual experimentation; the second is for the sex workers.

At first glance, this seems to counter the CCV. In reality, it does not. The young people have suburban, middle or upper class values, but are also seeking a thrill. They want something rough, something to challenge their bored existence. Not yet burned, they dance like moths around a flame. Traditional churches would fit into the same boring category as the rest of their lives; the outreach center's bold themes and in-your-face style are congruent with the teens' values on risk, challenge, and experimentation.

Meanwhile, the prostitutes live in a world of immorality. Those seeking change, seeking an escape, are attracted by light. Earning their living in darkness and degradation, their longing for something pure and clean is congruent with the values expressed in the flowers on the tables where they can share a cup of coffee with a friend who cares.

Congruent Witness Observed

I have observed the congruence principle in many situations of witness over the years. I remember my mother describing, in the 1970s, American-style cooking classes offered to middle class Japanese women as a fruitful door opener for evangelism. In a 1980s Bible study among wealthy

Ecuadorians led by American missionary women, the participants were intrigued by American culture and eager to learn from their expatriate friends about cuisine as well as Christ.

Around 1980, while I was studying at the University of Colorado, I was involved in ministry with Max and Pat Kershaw of International Students, Inc. Max was a wonderful mentor, whether teaching me about sharing my faith or replacing my car's water pump on the street in front of my apartment. The Kershaws' home was frequently filled with international students. Nationality was obviously not a common factor, but the shared experience of being students, being away from home, and having a hunger for some sort of community and care brought them together and attracted some to Christ. Max and Pat's deep love for the students was congruent with the students' need for someone who cared, who could help them understand the perplexing things of American life, and who could provide a sense of family for them.

More recently, we have seen the phenomenal growth of sports ministries. When I was younger, the witness of a Christian sports star attracted me—and many others. Now many ministries find that it is not just celebrity but community sports that count, such as a sort of neighborhood Olympics, combining fun, competition, community development, and witness around the commonly held cultural values of sports. Even in refugee camps the value of sports ministry has been shown, as a simple ball and makeshift goal can be used to relieve boredom and release built-up tension.

In a more formal research setting, I interviewed all of the young men in two cities of an Islamic nation who were known to be followers of Jesus Christ. As they told me their stories of how they came to faith, I was particularly interested in the type of person who witnessed to them and how it related to their own cultural values. Many of the young men were distressed to be citizens of their nation and desired nothing more than to escape to Europe. (Once believers in Christ, though, almost all of them held a much more positive and patriotic attitude.) These men were quite likely to be drawn to the gospel through the witness of a foreigner. Those, though, who were content in their ethnic and national setting were far more likely to report that a fellow citizen was the key witness.

Congruence Applied to Witness

Gabriël Jansen observed a principle among Moroccans coming to faith in Amsterdam similar to that which I had observed. Although of the same country of origin, there was great diversity among the people he studied. Many Moroccans in Amsterdam are of the Riffi Berber people. Some have lived their entire lives in the Netherlands, while others are recent arrivals from North Africa. In developing an ideal team for ministry among them, Jansen states:

> Young Moroccans grow up in a multiethnic pluralistic urban context. Following the principle of congruence, they can best be reached by Christians from this same urban context. . . . At the minimum, one or two Moroccan or North African Christians with the experience of living in the West must be part of the team. They should have enough Biblical and missions education, and be able to communicate in Dutch and Moroccan Arabic. At least one of them would also speak Tarifit [the language

of the Riffi Berbers] and preferably French. The team would best include a Dutch person, and possibly some other immigrant Christians, for example refugees coming from Muslim cultures.[16]

Hannes Wiher, drawing on scholarship and his many years of service in Guinea, has developed a very helpful understanding of the conscience through the lens of shame and guilt orientations. He points to the continuity and discontinuity between the indigenous conscience, the missionary's conscience, and biblical norms, another example of the congruence principle applied. Wiher writes:

The content of every conscience is close enough to God's norms in order to be an initial reference point (Romans 2:1–16). In initial evangelism, the missionary should therefore speak of sin with reference to the indigenous conscience, particularly [the aspect] of their conscience that is in agreement with Scripture (Priest 1994, 309). Other areas should not be approached in evangelism but only after conversion in teaching and counseling. These are of great concern to missionaries but of little concern to the indigenous. Therefore, the message causes misunderstanding in the audience and represents a call to accept the culture of the missionary. People may refuse, because conversion would lead from their "familiar, successful, and good" culture to an alien, perhaps even seemingly immoral culture. Or they may choose to convert exactly because it is a conversion to another culture that seems preferable. A conversion would in this case not be based on conviction, but on opportunism. Conversion, which bypasses the indigenous conscience, may lead to superficial conformity or to compartmentalized conformity, that is, syncretism. The missionary would have to take the role of permanent policeman with the misunderstood new culture.[17]

GOD'S SURPRISES

I do not suggest that the Congruence of Cultural Values principle is the ultimate principle of Christian witness. In geometry the term *congruence* is precise; applying it to missiology, I have used it as a relative term. And yet I believe this principle can help us move beyond the problems of the Homogeneous Unit Principle—to which the congruence principle can be reduced in some, especially monoethnic, settings.

Further, what I have written is descriptive, not prescriptive. There is a strong probability that the principle is true, but there is always the "God factor" and the human factor. People do not always respond in predictable ways, and God uses unusual people to accomplish his purposes. One of my favorite examples of this divine sense of surprise and humor is his use many years ago of a young man, now an older colleague of mine, to lead a fellow student to faith. He, whose name is certainly not widely known, holds a very conservative view on the role of women in public ministry; she, whom he led to faith, has become one of the most highly respected female leaders among American evangelicals!

It is refreshing to remember that although our reflection and analysis is important, God often has a way of working that we would have never thought of.

6

WHO'S TO JUDGE? LOOKING IN FROM THE OUTSIDE

It was 1964 and Lyndon Johnson was president of the United States. I had just overheard something I was probably not meant to know. My seven-year-old horror was immense. I *so much* wanted Grandpa to go to heaven, and I had always thought he was a Christian—but someone had just said that my grandfather had voted *Democrat* in every election since 1932! In my youthful understanding of faith and politics, that pretty much sealed his eternal fate.

Fast-forward forty-plus years. Many of my European friends today wonder how so many Americans—who sincerely call themselves Christians—can vote *Republican* and still consider themselves to be serious followers of Jesus Christ!

So, is it possible to be a Republican or a Democrat and still be a Christian? What about being a member of the British Labour Party, the German Greens, or the Swiss People's Party? Of more significance, to what extent can people individually and as a group be faithful in following Jesus Christ while maintaining social, cultural, and even legal identity as adherents of the religion into which they were born? Is it legitimate for a person born a Muslim, but now a true believer in Jesus Christ, to pray at the mosque although now praying in the name of *Isa al Masih* (Jesus the Messiah)? Or think about a European who has come to saving faith. Can he or she continue taking Communion in the nominally Christian state church where he or she was baptized as a baby by a priest or pastor who denies core elements of biblical truth? Is there a place for such believers to remain in those social and religious structures as a witness to Jesus Christ?

Lived-out faith will impact all of our lives, but does it require us to break all of our social ties and cultural practices? Could it be that we question the faith of others who do not break such ties on grounds just as flimsy and superficial as my seven-year-old understanding of my grandfather's voting record? We run the danger of making such judgments (for such they are) while failing to discern the complexity of life issues involved, not recognizing that we ourselves may be standing on sand, not on a rock.

CHANGING THE CHANNEL

Sadly, inquisitions, excommunications, and just plain, pride-rooted meanness have through the centuries caused unnecessary division in the church. Doctrine, *sound* doctrine, is important. Discerning between sincere brothers and sisters in Christ and "wolves in sheep's clothing" (Matthew 7:15; Acts 20:29–30) is vital. The time may come even to expel from the church a wicked person (1 Corinthians 5:13). Here I am speaking about something different.

In the early 1980s I served as personnel director on OM's ministry ship *Doulos*. Two young men came to me for a time of individual evaluation before returning to their homes in Argentina, their period of service on board completed. What had they learned? Among other things, one, from a Brethren assembly, said, "I realized that you can be a Pentecostal and be a real Christian." The other, a Pentecostal, had learned that "there are real Christians in the Brethren assemblies." Fortunately, in Argentina, Germany, the United States, and numerous other countries where such "family feuds" were intense and common, the withering attacks across the divide of the Spirit have tapered off in recent years.

Perhaps I am concerned about this issue because I have grown accustomed to being a "heretic," or at least called one by those faithful to the state religion where I have lived. Growing up in Colombia in the 1960s, I had no doubt that the dominant Roman Catholic Church considered *evangélicos* (Protestants) as outside the fold. So when things began to change after the Second Vatican Council and, for example, my parents were involved in a Bible study led by a Catholic businessman and his wife and another study frequented by a nun, eyebrows were raised—not in this case just by the Catholics, but by some Protestants puzzled at the thought that one could be a true follower of Jesus and yet remain in the Catholic

Church. (Of course some *evangélicos*, both Colombian and missionary, rejoiced over these developments, as did some Catholics.)

There are significant doctrinal issues over which I strongly disagree with Roman Catholics and Orthodox. (I could mention some concerns I have about certain teachings of several Protestant denominations as well!) And yet when an Orthodox friend says, in summary, "I am a sinner; I have no hope of eternal life except through the grace of the Lord Jesus Christ," how can I consider him as anything less than a brother in Christ? And if he *is* a brother, then should I not also treat him as one? Or will I continue to do what the hierarchy and law of his church do to me and other evangelicals: brand us as heretics? I will admit, though, that it is far easier to write these words than to live them.

It is not just our exclusive pronouncements about others that cut people off, but also the way we live and demonstrate what we *really* believe (James 2:18). Irish rock star Bono (whose father was a Protestant and mother a Catholic) observed at the February 2006 National Prayer Breakfast in Washington that religion—my brand versus yours—too often gets in the way of what God really wants to do. He decided to change to a "channel" different from the normal structures of the church.

> I remember how my mother would bring us to chapel on Sundays . . . and my father used to wait outside. One of the things that I picked up from my father and my mother was the sense that religion often gets in the way of God.

For me, at least, it got in the way. Seeing what religious people, in the name of God, did to my native land . . . and in this country, seeing God's second-hand car salesmen on the cable TV channels, offering indulgences for cash . . . in fact, all over the world, seeing the self-righteousness roll down like a mighty stream from certain corners of the religious establishment . . .

I must confess, I changed the channel. I wanted my MTV.

Even though I was a believer.

Perhaps because I was a believer.[1]

CUTTING THEM OUT

Beyond the squabbles among those who already call themselves Christian, the global growth of the church has often raised questions of belonging, behavior, and belief for those coming to faith in Christ from other religious backgrounds. This is not a new issue. The book of Acts has several such stories, and I believe the Gospel of Mark reveals the apostle Peter's own struggles—long before meeting Cornelius (Acts 10)—with issues of uncleanness and with accepting that Gentiles, too, are welcome in the kingdom of God.[2]

In cases where Christians are cutting off one another, where is doctrine impacted by personal issues? I referred earlier to Argentine Pentecostals and Brethren. Many of the stories that I heard in that period about church division in Argentina were not so much discussions of theology but sad accounts of broken relationships, feuds that often had been

71

triggered by some reporting a special spiritual experience not shared by the rest of the church. In Colombia there were doctrinal issues separating Protestants and Catholics, but violent persecution certainly made it no easier for Protestants to be broad-minded regarding at least the *possibility* of being born again and remaining in the Catholic Church. Again I stress: doctrine is vitally important. But how many times through church history have doctrinal debates been poisoned by broken relationships? Too often division and exclusion have been the result not of godly, humble discernment but of arrogance and narrow-mindedness.

CAN WE TRUST THEM?

In recent years there has been discussion in some missions circles of a concept known as an *insider movement*, something that would fit in the category I referred to in chapter 4 as "congruent communities." Ralph Winter refers to this concept when he notes that, in some settings, "It may well be that the largest number of genuine believers in Jesus Christ do not show up in what we usually call Christian churches."[3] Frank Decker observed that these movements "are not intended to *hide* a believer's spiritual identity, but rather to enable those within the movement to *go deeper* into the cultural community—be it Islamic, Hindu, or Buddhist—and be witnesses for Jesus within the context of that culture."[4]

In a very helpful article that points to many of the key publications in the recent discussion of this issue, John and Anna Travis—who have played a key role in this discussion through their writings—state simply that "in spite of concerns that some may have on this issue, the fact remains that in a number of countries today, there are groups of Muslims who have genuinely come to faith in Jesus Christ, yet have remained legally and socio-religiously within the local Muslim community."[5]

I think that my first contact with an "insider movement" was in 1972 when my uncle, a veteran evangelical Methodist missionary to Brazil, took my parents and me to a gathering of the Word of God charismatic Catholic community in Ann Arbor in the US state of Michigan. No one called it by that term; but, at least in retrospect and through Protestant eyes, that is just what it was. As I remember it, the community was "insider" in that these people were *not* breaking ties with their Catholic cultural roots and families but expressing their love for Jesus and joy of the new life he had given them in that social context. It was also "insider" in that the driving (human) force behind it was Catholic, not Protestant (although Protestants like my uncle had warm links with the movement). And it was a "movement" in the way it spread and multiplied along natural lines of social relationships with little overt organization or structure.

Eight years later, while in graduate school at the University of Colorado, I spoke at a missions conference in Denver. During a coffee break a veteran SIM (then known as the Sudan Interior Mission) missionary told me of an exciting movement among a Muslim tribe of Nigeria. Few, if any, Christians had ever gone to witness to that Islamic tribe, but some of their religious leaders had become intrigued by Isa al Masih as he is described in the Qur'an. Through that reading they had recognized his superiority and wanted to follow him, and they were desperate for someone to come and teach them more. They had not left their cultural ways and had not renounced Islam as such, but as a group many of them had turned to Jesus.

About the time I heard this story, Lutheran missionary Herbert Hoefer was discovering that in the southern Indian state of Tamil Nadu "there are thousands of people in the cities, towns and villages of India who believe solely in Jesus Christ as their Lord and Saviour but who have no plans to take baptism or join the church."[6] Hoefer pointed to the close association in Indian tradition between religion and culture and stressed the vital importance of community and family. Getting baptized and becoming formally associated with the established church would sever these "non-baptized believers in Christ," as he referred to them, from community and family.

"But are they *truly* saved, *truly* born again?" many of us ask. Somehow it seems a bit substandard, not fully *Christian*.

"These people," reported Hoefer, "have *experienced the love and power* of Christ in their personal lives," for which they have a "sense of *gratitude and faithfulness*" like the "one in ten who have returned to fall at His feet to say thanks." Typically they are "marked by a *reflectiveness and spirituality which* are [at] a considerable level above the ordinary, whether in the church or in society," and "are able to stand firm in this conviction with varying degrees of strength and steadfastness."[7]

This Indian movement, and Hoefer's book, raise significant questions. But the godly devotion of these men and women outside the fold of traditional Christian structures, and their commitment to Jesus Christ, outshines the spiritual life of many among us who, from a distance, might question the orthodoxy of their faith.

Lest anyone reading this chapter miss one of my key points, let me say again that sound doctrine is vitally important. In affirming at least the broad sweep, if not every detail, of what Hoefer has reported, I am *not* speaking of an inclusive approach that finds a basis for salvation in other religions or a means of being set right with God without the cross of Jesus Christ.[8] Nor do I question the vital importance of fellowship within the church. For these Indians, fellowship may not be in the *institutional* church but in other groups and relationships. The situation they face in the villages and cities of southern India is also significantly different from that of some "Christians" in my own country who have cut off relationships with other Christians due to a real, or just perceived, personal offense, or perhaps because they are simply too lazy or too proud to make the effort to find fellowship in a church.

Some readers (especially those who have not gone through Hoefer's entire account) may question the abstention from baptism. Baptism is important; it is a right and a privilege of all who believe (Acts 10:47) and an element of Christ's Great Commission (Matthew 28:18–20). Baptism symbolizes salvation and demonstrates identification with the people of God. If, however, we insist *too* strongly that these Hindu-background followers of Jesus be baptized, we may find ourselves slipping into the waters of "baptismal regeneration," the belief that baptism (and, to be on the safe side, baptism in *our* church) is an absolute requirement for salvation.

APPROPRIATE EVALUATION

One danger in our evaluation of such movements is an un-critical, "anything goes" approach to spiritual and ecclesiastical innovation. We, like the early church, must be graciously on our guard. When news of the new movement in Antioch reached the church in Jerusalem, the leaders, having a healthy concern, sent Barnabas to investigate (Acts 11:19–26). From Jesus' teaching, the church leaders already knew that false teachers would abound and that many would follow them (Matthew 7:15; 2 Peter 2:1–2). But can you imagine what would have happened to the young movement at Antioch if, instead of Barnabas, the apostles had sent some of the be-lieving Pharisees who later spoke up at the Jerusalem council (Acts 15:5)?

Barnabas was an encourager. A man of discernment, he did not pose a doctrinal exam but looked for "evidence of the grace of God" in the new movement among the Gentiles in Antioch (Acts 11:23). By comparison, some Christians today seem more like the Jerusalem council Pharisees (believers, but still Pharisees) in their response to some new movements God is bringing about today. Their attitude is captured in the cover of the *Mission Frontiers* issue I mentioned earlier in reference to the article by John and Anna Travis: a frightened, nail-biting young woman seems to be thinking the words of the cover's bold question, "Can we trust insider movements?"[9]

That journal cover points to three key issues in this debate.

First, we are often *afraid of what we do not know*. I have listened carefully when concerns about these movements have been expressed by people who have significant on-field experience and an in-depth understanding of the social and religious factors involved. However, when some others have spoken out or written from a distance, despite their general theological acumen and even missionary commitment I have wondered if they actually *know* these movements and the people involved, or only *know about* them. Especially when our firsthand experience is limited, we need to be humble (but never gullible) listeners.

Second, there is the danger of *unfair judgment*. Can a European or North American truly understand the issues of Indian social life? Can a Brahmin (high caste) background Indian know in depth the concerns and values of a Dalit (untouchable)? Can a Westerner raised in an environment stressing individualism and personal freedom comprehend the social pressures of a Muslim or Buddhist villager of Southeast Asia? In part, *yes* we can know and understand; cultures are not incommensurate. We can at least *partially* understand *if* we listen. But judgment on the issues I raise here is often premature because, as outsiders, we do not understand sufficiently.

Third, we run the risk of *assuming that we are "Jerusalem,"* that *we* are the ones with a special role of determining orthodoxy. I believe that the apostles and the leadership of the church in Jerusalem had a special responsibility in those early days. Today, though, while godly leaders are to be respected, biblically grounded theologians given a hearing, and the lessons learned by the global and historic church not to be ignored, we must humbly admit that none of us has a pope-like prerogative of judgment over the beliefs and practices of other followers of Jesus.

"GO HOME TO YOUR FAMILY . . ."

Mark 5 tells the story of the man possessed by a mob of demons named Legion. After crossing in the boat through the life-threatening storm, Jesus had arrived with the disciples on the east side of the Sea of Galilee, the Gentile region of the Gerasenes. There they were met by a tragic man, cut off socially and spiritually from his people by his demonic violence. Even after seeing the results of the man's deliverance, the people pleaded with Jesus to leave them.

As Jesus prepared to sail away, "the man who had been demon-possessed begged to go with him" (Mark 5:18). Whereas Jesus had called Simon, Andrew, and Levi with the words "Follow me" (Mark 1:17; 2:14), he said to this Gentile, "Go home to your family and tell them how much the Lord has done for you, and how he has had mercy on you" (Mark 5:19).

Why did Jesus do this? One reason is preparation. At this point the Gentiles of the region rejected Jesus and pleaded with him to leave. In the days following, on hearing the delivered man's story and how much Jesus had done for him, "all the people" in the Decapolis "were amazed" (Mark 5:20). Some time later Jesus returned and the people's response was much warmer. When he healed a deaf and mute man, the

Gentile crowds said, "He has done everything well" (Mark 7:37). It is also significant that "during those days" the second miraculous feeding took place, this time involving what I understand to be a *Gentile* multitude (Mark 8:1–10).

But there is another reason Jesus told the delivered demoniac *not* to come with him. The Pharisees were frequently challenging Jesus on the Jewish law and issues of uncleanness. Even his close followers had not yet understood that true "cleanness" is a matter of the heart (Mark 7:14–23), much less that God's plan included the Gentiles *as Gentiles* and not as proselyte converts to Judaism. In other words, at this point it would have been virtually impossible for the man to have accompanied Jesus without having gone through ritual conversion to Judaism.

Jesus, significantly, tells him not to join the band of his followers but to go home to his family. He is telling him not to convert to Judaism, not to go to the temple in Jerusalem or to a priest. He tells him to go home, to go back to his family, and to tell them what "the Lord" had done and of his mercy. Not to be confused with Jesus' later call to forsaking family *in terms of discipleship and commitment* (Mark 10:29–30; cf. the earlier statement in Matthew 10:37–38), Jesus here is telling the man that he can follow him *as a Gentile*, without breaking the ties to his family and society that would have come through conversion to Judaism.

So, what does the story of the Gerasene demoniac have to do with insider movements? First, we should note that, some years after this incident, the main emphasis of the Jerusalem council's conclusion (Acts 15) and a central theme of Paul's letter to the Galatians has to do with God's acceptance of the Gentiles *as Gentiles*, without them legally or ceremonially becoming Jews. Second, although Paul discusses the practices of other religions—for example, dealing with questions of what a believer could appropriately eat, not in terms of ceremonial cleanness but in association with idol worship and sacrifice (1 Corinthians 8; 10:14–22)—we need to be cautious in extending God's acceptance of the Gentiles *as Gentiles* to God's acceptance of practices, beliefs, and allegiances associated with their (or our) religions.

Given that caution, though, I reiterate that the story of the delivered Gerasene demoniac points to Jesus' authorization for that man to *not* become part of the group publicly known as his followers, to *not* become a Jew. Instead, Jesus wanted him to maintain his existing family and social relationships with the purpose of telling them of the things that God had done for him and of his mercy (Mark 5:19). Is it, therefore, stretching things too far to suggest that Jesus might today similarly authorize at least some new believers in some settings to *not* become a member of the community identified in religious terms as "Christian," to *not* take on "Christian" cultural practices and names that rupture existing social ties— with the purpose of telling their "family" how much God has done for them and of his mercy? And could it be that God is actually doing this because some ethnic, social, and religious groups will never understandably hear such good news if it comes to them in "outsider" forms and is told by "outsider" tongues?

GOING TO SOMEONE ELSE'S FAMILY

Concern has properly been addressed about the issue of what a missionary, an outsider, can properly *become* for the sake of witness. One significant concern is that we must always speak with integrity and not in any way use deception (2 Corinthians 4:2). Related to this is the concern that missionaries should not falsely give the impression to the people among whom they live that they have in some way converted to their faith. This is significantly different from the question of the ongoing cultural and social identification of a new believer from that group.

A full discussion of this significant issue goes well beyond the scope of this book; I do not intend to fully answer it here, although those who intend to serve in certain missionary settings *do* need to pursue the issue in depth. Let me simply comment that when Paul wrote that he had "become all things to all men" he tells us that his motive was "for the sake of the gospel" and that he might "win as many as possible" (1 Corinthians 9:19–23). Paul affirmed that he was a Jew (Acts 21:39) but recognized that his old, Jewish law-based righteousness was rubbish compared to knowing the Lord Jesus Christ (Philippians 3:7–11). He does not deny certain advantages of the Jews (Romans 3:1–2) but points to the equal sinfulness of Jews and Gentiles (Romans 3:9) and the equal access of Jews and Gentiles to God through Jesus, not through the Law (Ephesians 2:11–22). Paul was willing to give up or to take on certain behaviors and practices: to eat with Gentiles (Galatians 2:11–14) and to consume meat offered in sacrifice (1 Corinthians 10:31) yet without becoming an idol worshiper, to participate in Jewish purification rites (Acts 21:26) but with no indication that he (after coming to faith in Jesus Christ) offered any sacrifice at the temple.

Paul's identity by birth and upbringing expressed in his long years of ministry, then, is *both* that of a Jew and also that of a citizen of Rome (Acts 16:37; 21:39; 22:25). Although he might have eaten meat that had been offered in sacrifice, he never refers to himself in any way as an adherent to or participant in another religion. More to the core of his being and identity, though, is what he had *become*, described frequently as a "servant of Jesus Christ" (1 Corinthians 4:1; Galatians 1:10; Philippians 1:1). I suggest, then, that Paul's self-identification and intercultural practice as here briefly summarized point to what should be our emphasis and our limits: missionary outsiders who *identify with* the people we serve while maintaining a clear *identity in* the One we serve.

LOOKING FOR SIGNS OF GOD'S GRACE

So when it comes to insider movements, how do we respond? Discuss them? Yes. Engage them? Of course—with a humble, servant's attitude. Endorse them? At least in some cases, that could well be the proper response. But are we to judge them? I have come to the conclusion that *that* is not our task.

Instead, while we should not naively accept all that we hear of "movements of God" around the world, we should, like Barnabas did at Antioch, graciously look for evidence of the grace of God. Although the forms these signs of God's work take might not be quite like they appear "back home," such evidence will be found in four core areas:

- Belief in and witness to the resurrected Lord Jesus Christ (Romans 10:9)

- Study and application of the Word of God (Acts 17:11)

- People being transformed into Christ's likeness (2 Corinthians 3:18)

- A sense of being the body of Christ (1 Corinthians 12:27) and the people of God (Titus 2:14)

Not all who are "in Christ" will express their faith in the same way that you and I do. They may not become part of the same structures of the church to which we belong. The journey of some may be quite different from ours as they remain inside the social and even the religious structures into which they were born. But if they have truly heard "the good news about the Lord Jesus" and turned to him, let us be like Barnabas, who "was glad and encouraged them all to remain true to the Lord with all their hearts," with the result that "a great number of people were brought to the Lord" (Acts 11:20–24).

7

WORTHY WITNESS

"Hello, Mrs. Morrison. It's me, James."

The sixth grade teacher could hardly recognize the university student who spoke to her. His appearance was so different from the usually somber face of the boy she had taught eight years before. James had been something of a class reject; few wanted to be his friend. He was interested in science fiction and found joy talking about *Star Trek* television reruns with his teacher who, unlike his classmates, accepted him for who he was.

As he progressed through high school, James made an annual trip to his old school to visit Mrs. Morrison. Because of the age of the children she taught, and limited by state school board restrictions, she found ways to make sure her students knew of her faith but was careful not to abuse her position or violate the law. But when James tracked her down at a new school to celebrate his high school graduation, it was time to offer the young man a special gift—a Bible.

James was puzzled that Mrs. Morrison would give him such a gift. His family, angered at some incident in their congregation, had abandoned the church when he was a young boy. Because he valued his former teacher's friendship, he kept the book, although he put it away—out of sight and out of mind.

As James' university career progressed, new friends began to tell him of their faith and encouraged him to join with them in following Jesus Christ. The Bible was pulled from its hiding place, his teacher's kindness was remembered, and in time the Spirit of God transformed him.

Yes, the teacher realized, it *was* James. Over the years the young boy had become a man. More recently he had become a *new* man, a follower of Jesus won through patient, worthy witness.

COMFORTING WORDS

"Preach the gospel at all times—if necessary, use words." A comforting thought uttered, many say, by Francis of Assisi 900 years ago.

Too comforting.

Despite spending well over half my life with Operation Mobilization, a mission noted for evangelistic outreach, my natural tendency is to keep quiet and hope my light is shining. But Arthur Glasser reminds us that "evangelization of the world is a matter of both words and activity. It cannot be reduced to mere presence without dismissing all the valid data in the New Testament about imploring people 'on Christ's be-half: be reconciled to God.'"[1]

What should I do? If I had put into evangelistic practice on the Mediterranean island where we lived for many years the sentiment of a prayer I heard there, denouncing the "beast" of the state religion, my wife and I would soon have been look-ing for a new country of residence! The kind of action my acquaintance prayed for fits neatly, and correctly, into what the Middle East Council of Churches, and others, has labeled with the dirty word *proselytism*.

Unfortunately, though, in the region where I lived for several years virtually any form of evangelism is labeled "proselytism."

PROSELYTISM, ORTHODOXY, AND EVANGELICALS IN THE MIDDLE EAST

Scottish scholar David Kerr, with the commendation of Gabriel Habib, former General Secretary of the Middle East Council of Churches, deals with proselytism from a Middle Eastern perspective. Kerr refers to a 1989 MECC study docu-ment that looks at proselytism in terms of the historical ap-proach of the Catholic missions of medieval times and later Protestants, as well as contemporary "sects" (MECC's word), by which the MECC means

> millenarian or messianic groups, independent "neo-missionary" groups of fundamentalist persuasions, groups that represent syncretistic forms of religious universalism, charismatic renewal movements within

established churches, and new religious movements that claim to draw upon Asian forms of religious spirituality. While proselytism in West Asia/North Africa occurs unconsciously as well as consciously, its underlying presupposition is that a missionary "vacuum" exists throughout the region, where indigenous churches are considered to be lacking missionary motivation and resources.[2]

It is evident that, even with good intentions, a great gap of understanding exists. What one group might define as seeking spiritual renewal, another group calls "proselytism." As Fuller Theological Seminary professor Cecil Robeck points out, "Those who use the term [proselytism] have defined it *for* evangelicals rather than *with* evangelicals."[3]

George Sabra, a Lebanese Protestant theologian, provides a challenge that may help point the way ahead:

> To bring about a change, evangelicals must learn not only to respect their Orthodox sisters and brothers in their different traditions but also to work with them in witnessing to the gospel and speaking the truth to the world. Evangelicals must come to recognize that not all non-evangelicals are "nominal" Christians.

> For their part, the Orthodox must make a place for non-eastern Christianity, i.e. evangelical Christianity, as an expression of world-wide Christianity, and not simply as a foreign transplant in their "territories." Some Orthodox in positions of intellectual and ecclesiastical leadership should abandon the notion that individuals born in a certain religious community are the exclusive property of that community.[4]

"RICE CHRISTIANS" AND FORCED CONVERSION?

I remember something that Dr. Lionel Gurney, of what was then called the Red Sea Mission Team, said at a leadership development retreat in Germany in 1982. He described a mission hospital in a country known for its opposition to Christianity. Seeking to avoid any semblance of "paid conversions," hospital policy, he told us, was to dismiss any local staff member who became a Christian! Some might question this policy as being too harsh. But the problem of "rice Christians" is real.

At times, criticism comes from other Christians. I know of a situation that some describe as a major breakthrough in a specific people group turning to Christ—while others interpret the "conversions" as a pragmatic way to put a bit more food on the table. Such criticism runs the danger of turning into a withering "friendly fire"; but raised and responded to appropriately, it can help produce a mature church.

More often, the criticism comes from those outside the church. Even the popular *Lonely Planet* guidebook series considers the topic fair game. Referring to Cambodia's history, the refugee crisis of the 1980s, and the country's current religious situation, the travel guide states that "a number of food-for-faith type charities set up shop dispensing Jesus with every meal. Many Cambodians changed their public faith for survival, before converting back to Buddhism on their departure from the camps."[5]

Clearly the author has failed to perceive much of what God is doing in that land. But even so, he touches a spot where compassion and discernment may pull us in different directions, a topic that *should* be sensitive.

Elsewhere in South Asia, recent attacks have been more vitriolic. For many years, an outward aspect of tolerance characterized Christian-Buddhist relations in Sri Lanka, but underlying tensions have erupted into frequent violent acts against Christians in recent years. In a particularly tense time at the end of 2003, a leading Buddhist prelate died while being treated in a hospital in Russia. Rumors of Christian complicity abounded.

The editors of the online news service *Lankaweb* cautiously warned against an unrestrained backlash. They recognized the "predominant representation" of Roman Catholics among Christians and the "long standing recognized and respected existence" of Anglicans, Methodists, and Baptists in their country, and noted specifically the Salvation Army's compassion and care "towards people in distress irrespective of their faith." But the writers used the moment to lash out at the growing, newer churches.

> Over the past few decades there have however been incursions of fundamentalist Christian Sects propagating their unsavoury presence within Sri Lanka using proselytistic and forcible conversion tactics and many incentives backed by the riches imparted from their home bases overseas to lure persons into their communes. . . .

> While the need to exercise caution in the prevailing religious unrest within Sri Lanka is absolute and relevant matters [need] to be dealt with wisely and prudently to sustain the integrity of the officially recognized

denominations of Christianity in Sri Lanka, it seems also necessary without evil to rout [*sic*] out and disperse the unnecessary growing presence of the fundamentalist Christian Sects who persist in proselytism and forcible conversions in order to ensure peace and harmony in Sri Lanka.[6]

Neville Karunatilake, spokesman for the Sinhala Urumaya Buddhist Party, may have more fully exposed the goal. "We will not allow Christians to convert Buddhists to Christianity," he declared. "Conversions are unethical. We will stop them."[7] Following the religious component of the 2005 presidential elections and progress of the on-again, off-again anti-conversion law in Parliament reveals how deep-seated this issue has become and why it is of vital concern to Christians of Sri Lanka.

Reading these anti-conversion sentiments tends to shock us—at least those of us living in more protected environments characterized by a greater degree of legal and social freedom of choice. Use of terms such as *forced conversion* is upsetting, as is a misrepresentation of legitimate Christian charity. We *must* carry out such service, in line with the apostle John's forceful argument against any attempt to separate love for God and love for our fellow humans—in word and in deed (1 John 3–4).

On the other hand, do *we* rejoice when Christians, even those we might label as "nominal," turn to Islam, Buddhism, or newer alternative religions? We also respond with concern to conversion away from our faith to that of others and may complain, "Why should we allow them to build their mosques or temples in our country when we are not allowed to build churches in their country?"

Elsewhere we will look at social aspects of conversion that help to fuel opposition. But even accepting the fact that there will always be some opposition, even to ethical Christian witness, how can we move forward?

AN EVANGELICAL STATEMENT ON WITNESS

As criticisms of evangelism flourish, the World Evangelical Alliance recently stated their opposition to proselytism—what John Stott called "unworthy witness." Citing a 1970 World Council of Churches and Roman Catholic Church study, the WEA notes: "Proselytism takes place (1) whenever our motives are unworthy (when our concern is for our glory rather than God's), (2) whenever our methods are unworthy (when we resort to any kind of 'physical coercion, moral constraint, or psychological pressure'), and (3) whenever our message is unworthy (whenever we deliberately misrepresent other people's beliefs)." Contrasting the key words *proselytism* and *evangelism*, the WEA declares that to evangelize is "to make an open and honest statement of the gospel, which leaves the hearers entirely free to make up their own minds about it."[8]

Even ministry following this definition, though, may well generate opposition.

HOW DO WE GO ABOUT "WORTHY WITNESS"?

A North African friend of mine was attracted by the word *free*. The advertisement said it was free, and it was from Europe, so that was enough for him to send in the coupon without checking the details. ("It" turned out to be a Bible correspondence course.) Was he misled, or through his own mixed motives did he misinterpret a "worthy" message that eventually drew him to Christ?

In a conversation about the ministry of the vessels of OM Ships within a community, ship director Mike Hey recently described a layered approach of ministry. It is something like a Christmas package. No deception can ever be involved, but the outer wrapping (public actions, activities, and appearance) stimulates interest that causes people to probe deeper, through the layers, until they find the gift inside—perhaps long after the ship has sailed.

Bertil Engqvist, director of the development agency Operation Mercy, told me that integrity is vital in service and witness through community development. If we enter a situation with a commitment to feed one thousand people, we should not feed only five hundred while taking advantage of the situation to evangelize. But if we fulfill our commitment to the host government and feed one thousand people—or more—then our words, carefully chosen, can combine with our deeds for "worthy witness."

In 2002 I taught in a Bible school in a country where, despite a tradition of tolerance and legal freedoms, Christians are under increasing pressure. As we discussed principles of

Christian communication, the young evangelists in the class told me that evangelistic methods used by some groups were unnecessarily confrontational and provocative. The students said that others, who have close links to foreign (especially American) methods and resources, could understandably be perceived by non-Christians as representing yet another ugly aspect of globalization. Later, mixed with the massive sacrificial and worthy effort of Christians in response to the December 26, 2004, tsunami were a few relief workers—unfortunately, widely publicized in the local press—who foolishly trumpeted their evangelistic purpose and, implicitly, their lack of understanding of the region.

In that 2002 classroom we concluded that despite some lamentable examples, evangelical Christian witness could be—and often had been—carried out in worthy, respectful, ethical ways. Nevertheless, some opponents could always find grounds to interpret acts of mercy as purchasing converts and a fair presentation of the good news as cultural imperialism.

INTOLERANT TOLERANCE AND
UNAVOIDABLE CRITICISM

Our era is characterized by a return to exclusive fundamentalism on the one hand and what Arthur Glasser calls "careless tolerance and religious relativism"[9] on the other. No matter what we do, no matter how we live our lives, as we speak of our faith in Jesus Christ some will accuse us of "unworthy witness." And—it hardly needs mention—in different settings and at different times, different people will respond to different approaches in different ways.

Are outsiders more likely to accuse us of "unworthy witness" if they sense we are trying to move people from worship in *their* building to worship in *ours*? Could one key to "worthy witness" be a focus on the Center, not the boundary? The cross is itself a stumbling block (1 Corinthians 1:23); we need not add more stones in the path (2 Corinthians 6:3), much less build walls or try to force people into a specific pattern or process of coming to faith. A focus on *whom* we worship, not *where* (John 4:20–23), may take away at least part of the unnecessary stigma of unworthy witness.

Who determines whether our witness is worthy? Our lives should, where possible, win the respect of nonbelievers (1 Thessalonians 4:12). But in the face of opposition, our witness—with or without words—must be true and spring from sound motives. Ultimately it is God who tests us, whose approval we seek (2 Corinthians 4:1–2; 1 Thessalonians 2:1–6).

8

FATHOMING THE UNFATHOMABLE

To ask or search I blame thee not, for Heav'n
Is as the Book of God before thee set,
Wherein to read his wondrous Works, and learne
His Seasons, Hours, or Days, or Months, or
Yeares . . .

The archangel Raphael, speaking to Adam

Paradise Lost[1]

A MYSTICAL, MIRACULOUS, MERCIFUL WORK OF GOD

Conversion, coming to faith in Christ, is a merciful act of the triune God. Paul summarized this wonderful transformation in his letter to Titus:

At one time we too were foolish, disobedient, deceived and enslaved by all kinds of passions and pleasures. We lived in malice and envy, being hated and hating one another. But when the kindness and love of God our Savior appeared, he saved us, not because of righteous things we had done, but because of his mercy. He saved us through the washing of rebirth and renewal by the Holy Spirit, whom he poured out on us generously through Jesus Christ our Savior, so that, having been justified by his grace, we might become heirs having the hope of eternal life. (Titus 3:3–7)

We cannot fully understand Christian conversion. It is a mystical, miraculous, merciful work of God. Coming to faith in Christ is not something that can simply be boxed away as a psychological phenomenon or a social function characteristic of certain societies, as some secular observers might suggest. It is something that can only be comprehended with the insight and revelation given by the Spirit of God (1 Corinthians 2).

In John Milton's *Paradise Lost*, Adam discussed the mysteries of the universe with the archangel Raphael before Paradise was lost, his understanding not impeded by the smog of sin. Though our vision is impaired, there remains in us a proper desire to fathom how the eternal crosses into the temporal in our justification and salvation, how the spiritual interacts with the social and physical as we come to and live out our faith in Christ.

This kind of desire to "fathom the unfathomable" and "know the unknowable" is a desire granted by God. The Teacher declared that God has "set eternity in the hearts of men; yet they cannot fathom what God has done from beginning to end" (Ecclesiastes 3:11). Centuries later, Paul wrote, "I pray that you, being rooted and established in love, may have power, together with all the saints, to grasp how wide and long and high and deep is the love of Christ, and to know this love that surpasses knowledge" (Ephesians 3:17–19).

Spiritual wisdom and biblical truth are the base on which we stand. Concepts from mathematics and the social sciences, though, can enhance our insight into conversion, even if, like Paul, we have to admit that our understanding may still be more like the view through first-century polished brass rather than the precise detail we can see with a highly reflective, silver-backed twenty-first-century mirror (1 Corinthians 13:12).

THE INTERFACE OF TIME AND ETERNITY

If I hold a ball in my hand and look at it, I can see *almost* half of the surface of the ball. The moon is far away in its orbit around the earth, but even when it is full and the night is clear, I can likewise only see a bit less than half of its surface. Without using mirrors or cameras, I would have to be an infinite distance away (and have a *very* good telescope!) before I could see fully half of the ball's or moon's round surface.

At times I wonder if looking at truth is a bit like looking at these spheres. Although God gives me *sufficient* understanding of truth, I can never comprehend it *fully* with my finite human mind. Recognizing this motivates me to seek humility along with certainty.

Perhaps a bit of "distance" and some good "mirrors" would help us resolve some of our theological debates. If nothing else it might diffuse some tension when we disagree on topics such as "election and free will" or when we differ in our interpretations of those portions of Scripture that describe what I might call "security of those who *have believed*" as compared to the "security of those who *are believing*." Or do we simply need to listen more closely to others who, from our own perspective, appear to be looking at the dark side of the moon? My intention is not to solve those conversion-related debates here, but perhaps my suggestions will help others in such theological discussion.

One of the missing ingredients in most discussions about God's working in conversion is an understanding of the nature of time, infinity, and eternity. Perhaps that is because infinity is such a tricky thing.

For example, let me put ten balls on a billiards table (a very big table!) at one o'clock, and then you shoot one off at one-thirty. At two o'clock I add ten more, and you shoot off another at two-thirty, and so on. I can prove to you that if we had nothing better to do and kept on playing into infinity (remember, it is a *big* table!) there would be *no* balls on the table, or an *infinite* number—depending upon whether I treat the question as the sum of an infinite series or as a probability problem.

Flatland, Edwin Abbott's nineteenth-century science fiction classic,[2] has helped me grasp something of the nature of eternity and how it intersects with time. In his novel, a three-dimensional sphere enters the two-dimensional world of Flatland, where social hierarchy is determined by the number of sides a being has. There is no concept of "up" or "down," and travel is accomplished by moving along the plane—like cut-out paper squares, triangles, circles, and pentagons we might lay on a piece of flat poster paper.

In the story, the sphere causes great discomfort as he tries to teach and finally demonstrate the nature of three dimensions to the uncomprehending Flatlander, his worldview threatened by the concept of a third dimension. By moving up and out of the plane, the sphere is able to reappear at another point in the plane without moving along the plane, demonstrating what otherwise could not be grasped. Demonstration, though, does not lead to immediate acceptance!

Moving back to the real world, from my house above the city I can see my children's school a few miles away. I can unfold a street map that describes the way I will drive, and then I can point to the symbols of the intersections I will pass. While I can quickly move a toy car on the map from where we live to the school, in reality I cannot just appear in the parking lot. I need to drive across town as my watch and my car's odometer measure my progress in space and time. Further, when I get home with my teens for lunch, in space I am back where I started (at least relative to the surface of the earth); but although I can reset the hands of my watch, there is no way for me to turn back time.

Time and space are real, but in eternity their boundaries are surpassed. Just as the sphere moved in and out of Flatland, God—not bound by time or space—can be present with me as I stand on my balcony and equally present with me as I drive into the school parking lot—in addition to all the while being with my children both in the classroom and riding home with me for lunch.

Conversion, coming to faith, is a process that takes place in time. Time and events are real, not illusory. We have to "drive the streets" of human existence to get to our destination. What I do matters; my actions and choices have consequences.

Meanwhile, God is equally present with me where I am and where I will be, at the beginning and the end. Those who try to limit him to the constraints of time are "badly mistaken" (Mark 12:27).

Such an understanding provides a hint for me of how God can know the future while my choices remain real and significant, how he can elect yet allow free will. This helps me see that it is important that I complete the journey, not just start out.

OBSERVING, LEARNING, AND MINISTRY

Although we may describe conversion in spiritual terms, it has clear social implications. Coming to faith in Christ affects the psychology of converts and the society in which they live. Those changes can be observed and described with tools from the social sciences. Elsewhere, Rick Love and I have referred to seven "lenses" that can help us better understand conversion: psychology, behavior, sociology, culture, spiritual warfare, the human communicator, and God's underlying role. None of these aspects gives us the full picture, but each emphasizes characteristics that get overlooked when we examine conversion from other perspectives alone.[3]

Properly understood and grounded in Scripture, these lenses (and others; we do not claim to have compiled an exhaustive list) can help us gain new insights into how God is at work in conversion. In turn, these insights can help us grow in faith and be more fruitful in our ministry.[4]

Recognizing Our Biases

Anthropologists have not always been known as humble people. In the early days of the science, researchers too often presumed that they could observe and describe a society from a neutral, unbiased position. More recently the discipline has recognized that just as in the physical sciences it is impossible to measure something without affecting it, in the social sciences observation affects both the observer and the observed.

Writing about conversion is no exception. Although I strive for objectivity, it is impossible for me to strip away all biases affecting insight and interpretation as I describe a person coming to faith in Christ—or turning away to Islam, New Age, or something else. At a minimum, I need to admit the limitations on my perspective. As I develop skills of research and communication, I should interact with others in a way that helps me recognize those biases, even if I cannot fully shed them.

A secularist may recognize that a person's life has changed but find it difficult to accept the spiritual aspects involved. If I describe my encounter with God and the power of his Spirit, the skeptic may try to describe the transformation in terms of emotions and psychology—anything but a divine encounter. On the other hand, I may have taken such a spiritual bent that I cannot accept a description of change that involves psychology, economics, or treatment of a hormone imbalance; to deny that it is "all of God" somehow seems to reduce the role of grace and faith.

A clear example of the potential for diverse interpretation, even conflict, due to our biases is provided in the various published descriptions of conversion from Islam. Ibn Warraq, a man who turned from Islam to no religious faith, writes: "Muslims who have converted to Christianity would be deemed, by Muslims who are now atheists and humanists, to have left one form of unreason only to adopt another. But what reasons do Muslim converts to Christianity give for their conversion? These converts evidently found something in Christianity that they felt was lacking in Islam."[5]

While commending the courage to turn from their original faith, and even understanding some of the motives to turn to Christianity, Ibn Warraq and other writers in the same volume differ greatly from me in interpretation. I rejoice with those who found faith in Christ and sorrow over those who turned to no faith. Ibn Warraq and his colleagues, on the other hand, consider that "when we are completely free from faith, guilt, and anger, we are ready for understanding the ultimate truth and unraveling the mysteries of life. . . . Truth is in love and in our relationship with our fellow human beings, not in a religion or a cult. Truth is a pathless land."[6]

I found Ibn Warraq's book quite valuable. Although I do not agree with many of the thoughts he and his coauthors put forward, they helped me look at myself and my views on conversion through *their* eyes, as their treatment of Christian believers is almost always presented in a polite, respectful style.

I was able to learn far more from this book than I would have from simply reading another analysis of conversion by a fellow evangelical Christian.

Moving from Description to Prediction

I have a friend who has a PhD in chemistry and is employed by a pharmaceutical company. As she and her team develop new medicines, they can do tests that enable them to accurately predict how their drugs will act on humans. There are always exceptions (just read the "side effects" section of the information sheet that comes with any bottle of medicine), but before they put a product on the market they have great confidence that their medicine will work and *virtually always* will work in the same way.

Similarly, NASA or the European Space Agency can launch a rocket from earth and, with minor course corrections, propel it into orbit around a distant planet or through the tail of a hurtling comet millions of miles away. Precisely designed equipment operated according to well-defined laws of physics make the satellite arrive on time and on target.

In national elections, pollsters can predict a winner—well, most of the time. India's 2004 elections demonstrate where they can get it wrong. Politicians frequently use the polls to modify their platform and positions and achieve a predictable result.

But when it comes to conversion, whether of an individual or a group, moving from description to prediction is a risky business.

Donald McGavran described the way people had become Christians in India. In some of their more excessive forms, those who followed him were subject to the accusation of pre-scription: follow these steps and a church will result. Many hail the research of David Garrison on church planting movements. David himself would caution that the factors he lists describe observed movements; simply bringing about the factors or engaging in the described activities will not in and of itself cause a great turning to Christ.[7]

We need to recognize, first, the human factor. Humans do not always do what we expect them to do. Second, we need to remember the God factor. God does not always do what we expect him to do.

If studies of how people *have* come to faith cannot tell us how people *will* come to faith, of what value are they?

First, they can help us see tendencies in how people are coming to faith, which may encourage us to follow certain practices. If, for example, we find that people in villages who go through the *Firm Foundations* chronological Bible storying program[8] before making a profession of faith are more likely to "stick" than those who do not, we would be wise to use that information as we develop our ministry. But we must remain cautious: the observed value of the course demonstrates a tendency, not a law.

Second, such studies can point to gaps in our outreach. After doing research in a country with very few Christians, I stumbled onto the absence of any oldest brothers among the believers. Asking a group of national leaders if this was the case across the country, they insisted it was an exception—then failed to name even a single oldest brother among the thousand or so believers of which we were aware. Awareness did not lead directly to conversions, but it at least pointed to increased concern and prayer for this key subgroup of society.

Third, well-designed studies help us move beyond simplistic approaches. Time and again we hear that literature, radio, satellite television, dreams and visions, or some other single pet item is the key to people coming to faith in some part of the world. Each of those elements is important; rarely does God use any of them alone. We need to learn how God is at work so that we can better combine the variety of tools that he has given to us, understanding their interaction and avoiding wasted resources.

Fourth, they may uncover areas in which we must encourage our brothers and sisters to faithfulness. One of the more frightening books I have read recently is William Hendricks' *Exit Interviews*, written about Christians who, "having grown disillusioned with the church and other institutions of Christianity. . . are now looking elsewhere to meet their deepest spiritual needs."[9] Hendricks tends not to point to major theological issues of apostasy but to the absence of simple deeds of encouragement and concern. My own studies in North Africa pointed to the lack of burden bearing (Galatians 6:2). Hearing my report, three national leaders told me, "You have confirmed what we feared all along"—a concern that caused them to work for change. When research reveals such shortcomings, we ignore it only at great cost.

Finally, such research must be grounded in the Word of God. No, I am not saying that the Bible is a social science textbook. And we must not confuse our *understanding* of the

Word of God—illumined by the Spirit but also read through the lens of our cultural and experiential "glasses"—with the Word of God *itself*. Discovering, for example, that many people report dreams, visions, healings, or prophetic words as contributing factors in their conversion experience may help free me from an anti-supernatural mindset; grounding in the Word of God will keep me from becoming preoccupied with exciting phenomena and displays of power, maintaining my focus on God himself.

SUMMING UP

Can we describe God fully if we simply come up with sufficiently complex doctrinal "equations"? Obviously not. No such "box" can hold him.

Can we predict with certainty the behavior of humans given enough analytical skill in the social sciences? Again, no. God-given freedom prevents such prescription.

But the social sciences, properly used, *can* help us understand the diversity of journeys taken by those who follow Jesus Christ. Similarly, certain mathematical concepts can help us understand the way the infinite, timeless God worked at the cross—and works our in our time-bound lives—his gracious gift of salvation.

9

CONVERSION, POLITICS, POWER, AND TRANSFORMATION

John Smith was a revolutionary. At least that was the charge. The sugar cane plantation owners of Demerara did not need his kind of preaching about social reform in their colony, now part of the South American country of Guyana. When twelve thousand slaves revolted in 1823, Smith was convicted of inciting the rebellion. The Wesleyan Methodist missionary's teaching of freedom in Christ, it was said, lay at the roots of the revolt. Smith died due to illness in prison on February 6, 1824. A royal pardon had been conveyed but reached the colony the day he died, too late to set him free from the squalid prison and spare his life. Nine years later slavery was abolished in the British Empire.

William Wilberforce bears the antislavery movement's place of honor in the history books and in the public monument of his tomb in Westminster Abbey. John Smith, by government order, was buried secretly in the night in a grave long-since forgotten. Banned from attending the burial, Smith's widow and a friend, accompanied by a freed slave, observed the interment while hidden in the tropical darkness.

James Montgomery appealed to God's sovereignty and justice as he described the death and burial of this man of common name but uncommon courage, righteousness, and social conscience.

> *Are these the criminals, that flee*
> *Like deeper shadows through the shade?*
> *A flickering lamp, from tree to tree,*
> *Betrays their path along the glade,*
> *Led by a negro;—now they stand,*
> *Two trembling women, hand in hand.*
>
> *A grave, an open grave, appears,*
> *O'er this in agony they bend,*
> *Wet the fresh turf with bitter tears,*
> *Sighs following sighs their bosoms rend;*
> *These are not murderers;—these have known*
> *Grief more bereaving than their own. . . .*
>
> *Not by the slave-lord's justice slain,*
> *That doom'd him to a traitor's death;*
> *While royal mercy spread in vain*
> *O'er land and sea to spare his breath;*
> *But the frail life that warm'd this clay,*
> *Man could not give nor take away.*

His vengeance and his grace, alike,
*   Were impotent to save or kill;*
—He may not lift his sword, or strike,
*   Nor turn its edge aside, at will:*
Here, by one sovereign act and deed,
God cancell'd all that man decreed.

Ashes to ashes, dust to dust,
*   That corpse is to the grave consigned;*
The scene departs;—this buried trust,
*   The Judge of quick and dead shall find,*
When things that Time and Death have seal'd
Shall be in flaming fire reveal'd.

The fire shall try thee, then, like gold
*   Prisoner of hope! Await the test,*
And O, when truth alone is told,
*   Be thy clear innocence confest!*
The fire shall try thy foes;—may they
Find mercy in that dreadful day.[1]

POLITICS, POWER, AND PUBLIC DECISIONS

When I "went forward" at the age of six in the Methodist church of a small American town dominated by a Christian college and seminary, the political balance of the nation did not tremble. In fact, I doubt that my coming to faith in Christ had the slightest impact on the mayor, school board, or even the local dogcatcher!

Living in Colombia, South America, not long after, though, I heard stories of a town drunk in an outlying village who was transformed by Jesus Christ. The combination of changed life and changed allegiance (*evangélico*, not Roman Catholic, with its associated social and political links) had the potential to cause a local earthquake.

We decry the idea of conversion for political reasons, changing religion to gain or maintain power like some medieval European kings. But coming to faith in Christ leads to a transformation that cannot be divorced from any aspect of life, politics included.

Politics, simply put, is the way decisions are made in a society and the way power is given to legitimately enforce them.[2] Politics, and its relationship to the twin concepts of governance (a recognized right to lead) and government (the structures of leadership), is a vital part of every culture.[3] Since Christian conversion must affect our entire worldview, by definition it must have a political dimension, even if the response is to withdraw from political processes.

CONVERSIONS WITH NATIONAL IMPACT

When Constantine professed faith in Christ seventeen hundred years ago, his political position allowed him to make, and enforce, decisions that radically affected society and the shape of the Christian church—for better or worse, depending on your school of church history. Charles Colson's conversion came in prison in 1973 after he lost his White House position of power, but his voice and pen have had a powerful impact on American politics over the thirty years since he came to faith.

When Matthieu Kerekou, the Marxist leader of Benin (a small country next to Nigeria), came to faith in 1991 it led to both personal and national change. David Kilgour, a Christian and a senior member of the Canadian parliament well informed on international affairs, noted that "Kerekou was a Marxist-Leninist military dictator for almost 20 years, but a financially honest one even though the national economy did not perform at optimum levels. While in that position, he became a convert to Christianity, which in turn convinced him in 1991 that he must call an election for his office. He did and lost. Because he had not looted the treasury, he and his wife worked and lived simply while out of office."[4]

Kerekou's reelection in 1996, the process by which that happened, and the way he led the country in his new term are a clear demonstration of the *good* political side of conversion, impacting society by generally wise decisions with the power to put them in practice.

NEW TESTAMENT POLITICS

The New Testament is no stranger to politics. Leaving aside for the moment the theological issues at stake, the crucifixion of Jesus was the outcome of political scheming by Jewish leaders and their manipulation of the Roman governor, Pontius Pilate. It even led to the reconciliation of two Roman political and personal enemies, Pilate and Herod (Luke 23:12).

In Paphos on Cyprus, Paul and Barnabas encountered Elymas, who opposed their witness to the Roman proconsul Sergius Paulus (Acts 13:6–8). Spiritual forces were at work, but Elymas feared that his political influence would be lost if, as actually happened, Sergius Paulus were to accept Paul's message.

In Pisidian Antioch and numerous other cities, Paul faced organized opposition involving the political elites of the city. His Jewish opponents "incited the God-fearing women of high standing and the leading men of the city. They stirred up persecution against Paul and Barnabas, and expelled them from their region" (Acts 13:50).

The Philippian city leaders were alarmed to find that Paul and Silas were Roman citizens and that they had denied them their legal rights in their arrest, beating, and imprisonment (Acts 16:37–38). Later Paul was protected by that same system which governed his treatment under detention (Acts 22:29) and the process by which he was judged (Acts 25:16–21).

At his trial Paul was not manipulative; he had genuine concern for Agrippa as a man who one day would stand before God. That same "*agape* love" concern extended from the king to the common soldiers and court recorders in the room (Acts 26:29). Yet it is hard to imagine that, in his defense and witness before King Agrippa and in his appeal to Caesar, Paul did not also have in mind the potential of their conversion to faith in Christ, these men of such enormous political power—or at least of their becoming tolerant *simpatizantes* like the Colombians I described in an earlier chapter.

CONVERSION, THREAT, AND RENEWAL IN SOCIETY

Why is it that minority tribes of Myanmar and northeastern India in large part turned to Christ, while the dominant majority peoples remained in their traditional religion? Why did Korea, the only Asian country colonized by a non-Western country, turn to Christ in large numbers during the twentieth century, while Japan, the former colonizer, did not? Why did ancient Buddhism fail to spread eastward into territories under Persian control? Why did Islam fail to take hold permanently in Spain, which it controlled for centuries, or spread into what is now eastern Indonesia?

No simple or single theory can explain such conversion dynamics. Apart from any social science perspective, we must also take into account the sovereign purposes of God. Robert L. Montgomery has made suggestions regarding the importance of large-scale or "macrosocial" relations that affect whether people in a society will tend to convert to a religion being introduced from the outside. His work, based not just on the spread of Christianity but also of Islam and Buddhism, can help us understand how God has worked in the past and will be of value as we consider mission in the future.[5]

The first of two key factors in Montgomery's theory is *threat*. If a society perceives itself to be under threat, it is likely to resist a religion identified with the threatening society. Even in the twenty-first century memories of the Crusades of long ago, campaigns motivated more by the lust for power and money than by any issue of faith, stand as a wall imped-ing Christian witness among Muslims.

While much of the world has a love/hate relationship with the West (eager to enjoy its benefits; hating its power), Christianity associated with Western "imperialism" is often resisted. Americans ministering in the Middle East frequent-ly are questioned about their country's policy regarding the Palestinians, Iraq, and other flash points, these policies being interpreted as Christian attacks on Muslim peoples. A loving Christian may find a way over the barriers; but nonetheless, these politically rooted barriers are there.

It is not just Muslims who have felt under threat, strength-ening their resistance to conversion. Sebastian C. H. Kim ana-lyzes in great detail the religious conversion debate in India since independence. The Indian government's official *Niyogi Report* regarding Christian missionary activities, published in 1956, placed emphasis on the argument that Christian mis-sionary activity was "motivated by the fear of the spread of communism" and was "part of a Western Christian agenda to further their influence in India" in the postcolonial world of the mid-twentieth century. Kim challenges Christians to take seriously the concerns of Hindus, yet in his tolerant approach writes that the commission's "findings pictured the issues as entirely political, and ignored the spiritual and religious di-mensions of conversion and missionary activities."[6]

Returning to Montgomery's theory, the second key fac-tor might be called *non-threat*, since "the religions that have spread often seem to have offered a resource to leaders or to people as a whole in resisting threats to continued existence,"[7] whether those threats are in the form of military or political challenges or simply instability and decay in the structures of society.

As applied to the complex Indian situation, Montgomery's theory helps us to understand the conversion movements among the Dalits, the "outcastes" of Indian society and Hindu religion. Finding no hope for change in Hinduism, the renowned lawyer and prominent "constitution maker" B. R. Ambedkar, himself a Dalit, announced in 1935 his intention to convert to Buddhism, a pledge he publicly fulfilled in 1956 shortly before his death.[8] As Montgomery might explain it, this Dalit leader found in Buddhism a resource for Dalits to resist the centuries-old threat from caste Hinduism and to enable the continued existence of the Dalits as a group.

In recent years, Dalits in large numbers have followed Ambedkar's example and converted to Buddhism, Islam, and Christianity.[9] The movement has spiritual vitality while bearing undeniable political implications as it affects the *whole* life of the individual convert, converts as a group, and, indeed, the whole nation.

Looking for historical precedent to better understand today's situation, Samuel Jayakumar makes the following conclusion from his study of the nineteenth-century "people movements" in southern India:

> A close examination of Christian conversion movements among the depressed classes reveals that the missionaries also did not understand conversion in terms of a passive religious act limited only to forgiveness of sins. In fact they viewed it in terms of what the missionaries called the active dynamic of God's wonder-working power. . . . Conversion empowered depressed classes to quit

Hinduism boldly and endure severe persecution and even death for the sake of the revolution wrought in their lives. Such a conversion never puts down the oppressed. It lifts them up and puts them on higher ground. It is a life with all its fullness and humanness and self dignity. . . . Conversion normally provided the Dalits with character formation and a change of world view, a healthy emotional condition and a new intellectual outlook. Conversion also caused revolutionary changes in the socio-economic and political beliefs of the converts.[10]

This *non-threat* attractiveness of the gospel and human witness can be seen in other settings. The Berbers of North Africa, especially the Kabyle, have often been noted as being more responsive to Christianity than the dominant ethnic Arab majority of the region. The largest evangelical denomination in Spain is a church of the minority Roma (Gypsy) people (although there are many places where their ethnic cousins are *not* turning to Christ). In some restricted Islamic settings, Asian household workers, drivers, and gardeners are the ones whose witness has the greatest impact, not higher-paid Western engineers and businessmen.

It would be false to conclude from these paragraphs that missionaries and Christian "tentmakers" from powerful nations should withdraw *en masse* and return home. Most *do* have a vital role! It would be equally wrong for such workers to continue in ministry without an honest assessment of their personal values as compared to those of God's kingdom and earthly kingdoms.

Note also that the application of Montgomery's "threat theory" does not pertain merely to Westerners. Indians can be seen as a threatening force by other regional countries. Egyptians may be perceived, in other Arab lands, as holding too much power. Nigeria's and Brazil's neighbors may think these dominant countries throw their national weight around too much. These biases affect diplomats and businessmen; missionaries from these lands—not just white-skinned North Americans and Europeans—must take heed as well.

AN UNAVOIDABLE ISSUE

We simply cannot avoid the fact: conversion has political aspects. Governments and entrenched religious powers often attempt to limit freedom, knowing that changes in faith commitment—from any religion to another, not just to Christianity—have the potential to reform society. On the other hand, political freedom is no guarantee that religious conversion will take place; consider the initially warm, then cold, response to the gospel in Eastern Europe just before and shortly after communist governments were replaced, compared to a decade later.

Once people come to faith in Christ, political issues often arise. On the Mediterranean island where I lived for six years, even dying becomes a political act, since very few plots remain in the only cemetery available for "heretics" like evangelicals.

In a North African country a few years ago newspaper articles sharply attacked the growing number of believers in

Christ. One brave young man responded in published letters to the editor, declaring that those who had left Islam to follow Christ were not traitors but deeply loved their country and were faithful to it. He asked why they could not at least be afforded *dhimmi* status, a protected albeit somewhat second-class status afforded Jews and Christians in traditional Islamic society.

Religious institutions are often bound together with political structures. Incredible pressure was placed on Japanese Christians during World War II to engage in Shinto rites that combined national loyalty with emperor worship. Those who refused suffered. More recently, when evangelical believers refused to participate in traditional festivals among the Saraguro tribe of Ecuador or villagers in the Chiapas and Oaxaca states of Mexico, the challenge was not just to the religious system but also to the interwoven structures of politics and economy.[11]

Such challenges to Christians are nothing new. Persecution in the Roman Empire was often linked to believers' refusal to worship the emperor, coupled with scandalous rumors and false accusations. Tertullian, writing in the early third century, countered that Christians were faithful to the state and among its best citizens. Tertullian would not call Caesar "god," but he would faithfully serve him as a human, God-appointed emperor. In his lengthy *Apology*, Tertullian wrote:

> Without ceasing, for all our emperors we offer prayer.
> We pray for life prolonged; for security to the empire;
> for protection to the imperial house; for brave armies,
> a faithful senate, a virtuous people, the world at

rest, whatever, as man or Caesar, an emperor would wish. . . .

There is also another and a greater necessity for our offering prayer in behalf of the emperors, nay, for the complete stability of the empire, and for Roman interests in general. For we know that a mighty shock impending over the whole earth—in fact, the very end of all things threatening dreadful woes—is only retarded by the continued existence of the Roman empire. We have no desire, then, to be overtaken by these dire events; and in praying that their coming may be delayed, we are lending our aid to Rome's duration.[12]

Don't misunderstand: I am not calling for churches to turn into political parties! Great caution is needed in some areas. The most obvious sensitive issue, and yet so difficult to deal with, is that of appropriate patriotism versus ungodly nationalism. It can be entertaining when you cheer for your country and I for mine in the Olympics or World Cup. There is a proper desire for our homelands to prosper and progress. Quite a different story is when your country goes to war with mine, or a war is perceived as a "Christian" attack on non-Christians. My concern applies not only to American and Western European use of military power but equally to the complex situations in Nigeria, Indonesia, the Balkans, Azerbaijan, Armenia, Russia, and Cyprus that have resulted in violence and military conflict between Christians and Muslims in recent years.

We must also be sensitive in how we discuss conversion and other faiths. While I hold that salvation is found only by faith in Jesus Christ and long for each person to have the privilege of a free, fair chance hearing of the gospel, this must be pursued with respect for those of other belief systems.

Gone are the days of private correspondence! What I write in a newsletter, speak from a pulpit, or publish in a journal today might be read tomorrow by anyone, anywhere, who has a computer and Internet access. Although some phrases may have an appropriate biblical context and usage, as emphasized at the June 2000 international "Consultation on Mission Language"[13] and reiterated four months later by a gathering of the Evangelical Fellowship of India,[14] now more than ever we need to be careful with militant and military language when speaking of people coming to faith. Terms such as *crusade*, *target*, and *spiritual warfare* should be used with caution, if at all.

Beyond speaking and writing with such words, we should examine our own hearts. Why do we use them? Are they merely expressions we picked up from Student Volunteer Movement songs of the early 1900s or the recent "strategic level spiritual warfare" thrust? Or is there an underlying attitude behind such words that needs to change, an attitude that reflects unbiblical political themes of domination and conquest rather than of humble incarnation and service?

TOWARD TRANSFORMATION

There are times when we need to follow Paul's example of claiming citizenship rights and enter into the legal and political process in a spirit of prayerful humility. Networks concerned for human rights have done much good in recent years in supporting Christians under pressure from intolerant governments. Prayer and quiet diplomacy generally are more helpful on these issues than public campaigns that tend to make it more difficult for the offending government to back down.

On the other hand, our choice may be one of withdrawal from involvement in the public square. Even that is political. As the Wheaton '83 Statement declares, "Our very non-involvement [in political action] lends tacit support to the existing order. There is no escape: either we challenge the evil structures of society or we support them."[15]

In Romans 13:1–7, a passage that I find hard to apply to countries ruled by tyrants, Paul instructs us to submit to the governing authorities and to pay our taxes, because all authorities that exist "have been established by God" (v. 1). Application of this passage today must look at both Paul's example and his teaching, which, for the community of believers in Thessalonica, would be demonstrated in brotherly love, a quiet life, commendable work, and appropriate independence—all of which would lead to respect by outsiders (1 Thessalonians 4:9–12).

Is there an underlying biblical theme that may help us define the appropriate political aspect of conversion, a theme that is valid at individual, local church and community, and wider levels? An increasing number of voices are using the term *transformation*. Not referring here to any organization that uses the word in its name, the concept involves both individuals and communities coming to saving faith in Jesus Christ and the displacement of evil structures and renewal of life in families, neighborhoods, and at times across towns and cities.

Chuck Van Engen notes that transformation involves both discontinuity and continuity. There is change, but not merely a change of religious affiliation, church membership, education, ethics, or politics. "Rather, a missiology of transformation entails the *new formation*, the *re-creation* of whole persons—of all and every aspect of their lives. . . . It has simultaneously personal, social, structural and national implications. It involves reconciliation with God, self, creation, others, and the socio-cultural structures."[16]

René Padilla, using the term *integral mission*, says that such transformation can only be carried out by an "integral church," a church that is not perfect but "making progress in its own transformation and the transformation of the community which it serves." It is a church that recognizes Christ's lordship over everything and everyone, sees Christian discipleship as a missionary lifestyle to which "the entire church and every member have been called," lives in a way that this confession of Christ as Lord "can be seen as the inauguration of a new humanity," and uses its gifts and ministries to fulfill its vocation as "God's co-workers in the world." The integral church "is one which recognizes that all spheres of life are 'mission fields' and looks for ways of asserting the sovereignty of Jesus Christ in all of them."[17]

Because true Christian conversion affects all aspects of our lives, it has political implications. At various levels of society it will affect the way power to make decisions is established and enforced. The personal transformation and escape from conforming to the world system Paul calls for in

Romans 12 helps define the nature of our submission to God-ordained authorities as required in Romans 13.

TRANSFORMATION FLOWS THROUGH TRANSFORMED PEOPLE

Transformation can only flow out of the lives of those who "with unveiled faces all reflect the Lord's glory, [and] are being transformed into his likeness with ever-increasing glory" (2 Corinthians 3:18). The passive voice of "being transformed" here and in Romans 12:2 does not indicate passivity but grammatically reminds us that we cannot transform ourselves. Transformation is something we receive from God. He is the beginning and source; his glory is our goal.

"Mission as transformation" is worked out in many forms, varying in expression from megacity slums to corporate boardrooms. I suggest, however, that whatever its location or outward appearance, in 2 Corinthians 4 Paul points us toward three nonnegotiable elements of biblical transformation.

Jesus-Centered Proclamation

Followers of Christ can applaud, and receive the benefit from, the progress made through God's common grace demonstrated in good government and philanthropic science. Faltering as it may be, progress is made and steps are taken to alleviate poverty, deal with disease, improve education standards, and even work for peace. Whether help comes through World Vision or the Red Cross, we rejoice when orphans are cared for and disaster victims find shelter.

Mission as transformation, though, begins with "Jesus Christ is Lord." Ultimately, apart from Jesus even the evident good of this world is perishing. Unbelievers' minds are blinded; they cannot see the "light of the gospel of the glory of Christ." As creation began when God proclaimed light into existence, transformation radiates from the Jesus-centered light in our hearts (2 Corinthians 4:4–6).

Jesus-Honoring Service

Not only is Jesus Christ Lord, but the complement of this truth is that "[we are] your servants for Jesus' sake" (2 Corinthians 4:5). This is not a type of service that somehow wins merit, which atones for our own—or others'—failings. It is service that, however expressed, is done for the sake of Jesus.

This kind of servanthood is not the stuff of an occasional sanitized, safe weekend trip to the inner city or a "clear my conscience" missions junket to some needy nearby land, the kind of "ministry" that is more about "me" than about service.[18] Servanthood left Paul hard-pressed, perplexed, persecuted, and struck down; feeling like a fragile clay jar; walking as one who always carried around in his body the death of Jesus (2 Corinthians 4:7–10).

Servanthood has its moments of joy, but at a price.

Jesus-Based Hope

Transformation ministry often deals with the "down and dirty" side of life, with people who are hurting, hopeless, and impoverished. We rejoice when a drug addict recovers, when a child learns to read, when bitter enemies say "I forgive." These things matter! We are not Gnostics who somehow pretend that this life and our physical bodies do not count. Yet, with Paul we admit that "if only for this life we have hope in Christ, we are to be pitied more than all men" (1 Corinthians 15:19).

But we *do* have hope, not just for this life but for a resurrection-based eternal life promised to us in Jesus Christ that is far beyond anything we can imagine. It is the hope of an eternal glory that far outweighs all of the disheartening, body-wasting, death-threatening troubles—"light and momentary troubles"!—with which we struggle (2 Corinthians 4:16–18).

NOTHING NEW

Transformation is *not* a new concept; it is as old as God's first gracious acts among men and women. It is something that has taken place over and over again as the gospel has spread throughout the centuries. And yet it is a vital *renewal* concept, something that God's people must take hold of again in the twenty-first century. It is a concept built on God's Word and on the premise that conversion is a matter that must transform you, me, and the church as a body at the deepest level of our being.

10

THE DEFEAT OF DARKNESS AND DECEPTION

I was ten years old. We were driving across Texas, heading home. Dad had stopped at a veterans medical facility to visit "Roger," an acquaintance with emotional as well as spiritual needs. My sisters and I sat in a hallway and entertained ourselves while Mom, Dad, and Roger talked in a private room.

It was summer, it was hot, and I thought I had more important ten-year-old things to do than wait in the hall reading a book. My patience having reached an end, I pounded on the door of the room where Mom and Dad were talking with their friend.

Mom slipped out and quieted me before I could voice my protest. She told me that just at the moment my patience had broken and I began drumming on the door, Dad had been concluding the conversation and inviting his friend to turn to Jesus as his Savior.

Not quite the stuff of a Frank Peretti novel, I look back on that "spiritual warfare" event with chagrin. Although I had given my heart to Jesus, that did not mean I had total victory over impatience and selfishness! In my sinful weakness, the devil manipulated me as part of his evil strategy to try to keep Roger in the kingdom of darkness.

NOT AGAINST FLESH AND BLOOD

Coming to faith in Christ is the result of a spiritual battle. Even if it is not a process filled with overt encounters with demons and breaking of curses, we know from Paul's letter to the Ephesians that "our struggle is not against flesh and blood, but against the rulers, against the authorities, against the powers of this dark world and against the spiritual forces of evil in the heavenly realms" (Ephesians 6:12).

Earlier in that letter, Paul had written, "You were dead in your transgressions and sins, in which you used to live when you followed the ways of this world and of the ruler of the kingdom of the air, the spirit who is now at work in those who are disobedient. All of us also lived among them at one time, gratifying the cravings of our sinful nature" (Ephesians 2:1–3).

These and numerous other Scriptures point to a key aspect of a biblical worldview: the reality of the spirit world. Too many growing up in the West have been oblivious to this cosmological fact. A number of leading writers in the 1990s "spiritual warfare" movement mentioned a personal paradigm shift—something that perhaps contributed to the excesses of the movement as they moved from ignorance of the reality of the spirit world to preoccupation with it.

By contrast, I find it interesting that among the American writers who, like me, early in the debate called for reality and balance in this field, some, like me, are missionary kids.[1] We grew up aware of the reality of demons and their influence, but were not preoccupied with it. As I remember Paul Hiebert commenting one day, like a basketball player on the court we see them in our peripheral vision, but our focus is on the goal, on Jesus. (I must admit, though, that when on Friday nights in the boarding school dorm certain missionary uncles told stories of demonic encounter in the Amazon, the impact was not one of peace, worship, and confidence in the cross! We had no doubt of the reality of the encounters; but the storytellers seemed to be telling us a sort of "action story" without pointing us to our assurance and victory through Jesus.)

The one true, triune God has created spiritual beings and human beings (who, of course, have body and spirit). We humans corporately form an inanimate world system, the society in which we live. The passages from Ephesians quoted above point to our own sinful human nature, the system of the world, and the spiritual forces of evil—all in rebellion against God. The trap of our sinful nature and desires is reinforced and energized by the impersonal "ways of this world" and the personal "ruler of the kingdom of the air" and the spiritual beings who serve him. One aspect of conversion involves recognition at the worldview level of these biblical, cosmological truths.

JESUS WON THE VICTORY!

Thanks be to God, we are not left to escape on our own! "For he has rescued us from the dominion of darkness and brought us into the kingdom of the Son he loves, in whom we have redemption, the forgiveness of sins" (Colossians 1:13–14).

Conversion depends on the spiritual battle that Jesus has won. Dr. Ed Murphy points out key past/completed, present, and future aspects of this victorious work of Christ.[2]

Jesus began his redemptive work and defeat of Satan by refusing to give in to the temptation to sin and the offer of a "cross-free" shortcut to glory, both in the wilderness (Matthew 4:1–11) and throughout his sinless life (John 8:29, 46). Delivering demonized people during his earthly ministry and granting authority to his disciples over the power of the enemy continued the defeat of the devil. The centerpiece of Jesus' victory over the devil was in his redemptive act on the cross and the fivefold event of his death, burial, resurrection, ascension, and glorification (1 Corinthians 15:1–8). The Lord Jesus maintains Satan's defeat and the believer's redemption through his ministry of intercession on our behalf at the right hand of God (Romans 8:33–34). He will complete the defeat of Satan and the redemption of believers at his glorious Second Coming (2 Thessalonians 2:8; Revelation 19:19–21; 20:7–10).

A DECEPTIVE ENEMY

Even though the battle has been, is being, and will be won, conversion is a spiritual battle—as the enemy conspires to deceive us in order to prevent us from understanding the truth and to keep us in his kingdom of darkness. It may be through the distractions brought about by an impatient ten-year-old boy; often it is through methods much more overt or, alternatively, much more subtle, sinister, and prolonged.

The overt method of devilish spiritual deceit is the method of Simon the sorcerer of Samaria (Acts 8:9–11) or of the apocalyptic beast that came out of the sea (Revelation 13:1–10). Both of these arrogant blasphemers created an awestruck band of followers through acts of sorcery and evil spiritual power.

The good news is that even a Simon can be set free, both then (Acts 8:13–24) and now! Although the relationship between this Simon and the first-century heretic "Simon Magus of later legend is not clear[,] Luke's statement about the Samaritans' veneration of Simon . . . seems to support the identification of these two."[3] If indeed the two men are the same, the Acts 8 story points to the potential of deliverance and conversion, and the extra-biblical material to the need not merely to come to the cross but to continue the journey.

Robert Moffat, father-in-law of the more famous David Livingstone, served under the London Missionary Society in southern Africa in the early 1800s. He led to faith in Christ a powerful chief known as "Africaner," a man who eventually served alongside Moffat. LMS worker William Swan, assigned to far-off Mongolia, heard of the conversion. Perhaps longing for more fruitfulness in his own ministry among shamanistic Buddhists and their powerful monks, he described Africaner's incredible transformation in verse.

There was a man whose very name once shed
The dews of death on every heart around;
With nightly draughts of reeking blood he fed
His glutton idol Murder. His soul found
Its solace in the wild distracted sound
Of parents shrieking for their children slain,
Of children wailing when the moisten'd
   ground
The blood of parents did with crimson stain;
   Destruction his delight, his pastime to give
   pain.

But now, he cultivates his peaceful vale!
Around him youth and age in safety sleep,
And hail him with a smile! This is no tale
Drawn from the records Monkish craft did
   keep;
For 'twas but yesterday the yesty deep
Convey'd the news that Africaner, now
Another man, doth pray, and love, and weep!
His heart is tamed, a calm sits on his brow,—
   The lion is a lamb!—Go, skeptic, ask him,
   how?

He heard the tidings mercy sent from heaven;
He heard, and, melted by the Saviour's love,

Cried, "May a murderer be yet forgiven?
Save me, oh Jesus, save!" while, like a dove,
Descending on the prostrate from above
The Spirit came: contrition's waters flow;
He reads the page of truth; his fears remove;
His faith and love with fairest blossoms blow,
Repentance bears her fruits, and bends her
branches low.[4]

C. S. Lewis described the covert side of devilish deception in *The Screwtape Letters*. In this book, the master demon tells his apprentice that if people will not believe and fear a real devil, then he should lead them to believe that the devil does not exist at all.

Such is the strategy of false teachers, the wolves we are so often warned against in the New Testament (Matthew 7:15; Romans 16:17–18; Colossians 2:4; 2 Peter 2:1; 2 John 7). The most dangerous of these teachers are those who "have secretly slipped in among you" (Jude 4). They are not nasty but kind, sometimes a sort of grandfather figure, the kind of person you feel you can talk to. "They are the kind who worm their way into homes and gain control over weak-willed women" (2 Timothy 3:6). After they have won the confidence of their hearers they slowly, subtly inject the poison of false teaching. When someone stands up to oppose the heresy, the response of the deceived may not be theological but personal: "But he is such a *nice* person! How could he be a false teacher?"

The man I met in Boulder, Colorado, in 1980 who claimed to be Jesus deceived few and did little damage, except perhaps to himself. People did not follow him; they laughed at him or perhaps pitied him. I cannot say the same about certain pastors, authors, and professors who "secretly introduce destructive heresies" (2 Peter 2:1) that have rocked the faith of those who trusted them.

As in military conflict, somehow the overt side of the battle seems easier to face than the covert—we clearly know who the enemy is and the position from which he is likely to attack.

CONVERSION INVOLVES A SHIFT OF ALLEGIANCE AND CITIZENSHIP

Finally, conversion is a spiritual battle that involves a change of allegiance that may include the breaking of overt demonic power in our lives.

Writing from third-century Carthage, a key center of the Roman Empire in the land we now know as Tunisia, Tertullian's *Apology* describes the activity of demons.

> Their great business is the ruin of mankind. So, from the very first, spiritual wickedness sought our destruction. They inflict, accordingly, upon our bodies diseases and other grievous calamities, while by violent assaults they hurry the soul into sudden and extraordinary excesses. Their marvelous subtleness and tenuity give them access to both parts of our nature. As spiritual, they can do no harm; for, invisible and intangible, we are not cognizant of their action save by its effects, as when some inexplicable, unseen poison in the breeze blights the apples and the grain while in the flower, or kills them in the bud, or destroys them when they have

reached maturity; as though by the tainted atmosphere in some unknown way spreading abroad its pestilential exhalations. So, too, by an influence equally obscure, demons and angels breathe into the soul, and rouse up its corruptions with furious passions and vile excesses; or with cruel lusts accompanied by various errors, of which the worst is that by which these deities are commended to the favour of deceived and deluded human beings, that they may get their proper food of flesh-fumes and blood when that is offered up to idol-images. What is daintier food to the spirit of evil, than turning men's minds away from the true God by the illusions of a false divination?[5]

In the Gospels, Jesus delivered many from demons, including his close follower Mary Magdalene (Luke 8:2). "Many" came to be delivered from demonic power (Matthew 8:16), but the need was not universal. We have no record of Peter, James, John, or the rest of the Eleven being delivered in the way Mary was.

Most followers of Christ I know have not suffered under, nor been delivered from, the dramatic manifestations described by Tertullian. A few have. Some of them have come from an Islamic context, such as the former village sorceress I met in Southeast Asia. The missionary who led the sorceress to faith expressed hope for others trapped by the devil when she wrote to her friends: "When I sit laughing with her, who used to be the most evil woman I ever met, and now is my closest friend, I know that nothing is impossible with this God we serve!"

A woman from a Buddhist background had trusted in Christ as her Savior and was serving him outside her home country. Even as a young missionary, she struggled with spiritual oppression. The source of her bondage was linked to curses pronounced on her as a baby. Eventually a small group prayed with her and over her, claiming Jesus' victory and freedom over the demonic powers that harassed her. Her deliverance was a dramatic event. It would be easy and even entertaining to focus on the strange things that took place in the room; I prefer to emphasize the victory that Jesus gave her that day.

Some years ago a martial arts champion in Europe offered his technical help to our team. He had turned to Christ, but there was still something evil about him that was triggered when he met certain people. Having confronted him after one unfortunate episode, I urged him to accompany me to visit friends experienced in deliverance ministry and seek God's help. He was eager to go. There were no shrieks, no raised voices, and no flying chairs, not even a clenched fist as we talked and then prayed. To win his matches he had invited spiritual beings to give him additional skill, speed, and strength. He renounced his allegiance to those evil beings, and we commanded them to depart in Jesus' name. Love flooded him, and indeed the whole room, as he was set free. Afterward we walked the downtown streets looking for a place to eat. People turned their heads to watch: there was something tangible about the Holy Spirit's presence in my delivered friend—a victory that lasted, as it was reaffirmed through a walk of discipleship.

Conversion involves a change of allegiance; a part of what is involved for all who come to faith in Christ. By his death,

Jesus destroyed "him who holds the power of death—that is, the devil—and free[d] those who all their lives were held in slavery by their fear of death" (Hebrews 2:14–15). God "has rescued us from the dominion of darkness and brought us into the kingdom of the Son he loves, in whom we have redemption, the forgiveness of sins" (Colossians 1:13–14).

Some, like Mary Magdalene and the martial arts champion, need a specific act of deliverance from demonic powers. Others, equally dependent on the cross, walk a different journey and may not require such specific ministry. Coming to faith in Christ for *everyone*, though, involves a change of allegiance from the "ruler of the kingdom of the air" (Ephesians 2:2) to the "eternal kingdom of our Lord and Savior Jesus Christ" (2 Peter 1:11). Continuing in that faith, even if overt demonic attacks are absent, involves an ongoing battle against the false teachers and devilish deceivers who attack the church and distort the truth.

A GLORIOUS HOPE

We have a glorious eternal hope whether the battle is hidden or obvious, theological or physical, even in the face of overwhelming odds.

Jude, who wrote clearly of the danger of false teachers and fallen angels, commands us to "build yourselves up in your most holy faith and pray in the Holy Spirit" (Jude 20). As we obey that command, our hope rests not on what we do but in the one who gained the victory for us:

To him who is able to keep you from falling and to present you before his glorious presence without fault and with great joy—to the only God our Savior be glory, majesty, power and authority, through Jesus Christ our Lord, before all ages, now and forevermore! Amen. (Jude 24–25)

11

BECOMING THE PEOPLE OF GOD

It was New Year's Eve, 1986, in Utrecht, Holland. Blustery and cold outside in the midwinter twilight, indoors the Jaarbeurs conference hall was pulsing with energy, spiritual energy. We were nearing the climax of Mission '87, a gathering of over ten thousand European students and young adults excited to find out how God is at work.

As I looked around the auditorium, I found it easy to identify national groups as the worship band led us into a time of praise. Many years later I cannot remember the specifics, but there was something that told me where different clusters of people came from: one long line swayed from side to side, arms around shoulders; others bounced up and down like toys with springs; and some, of course, stood erect, hands at their sides.

I was not (and am not) critical of the differences in worship style; the variety enriched our celebration. Somehow it seemed to be a time-bound preview of what John describes in Revelation 7:9–10: the spectacular scene around the throne of God as an uncountable multitude cry out praises. John does not go into detail, but in my mind I imagine these people from every nation, tribe, people, and language joyfully worshiping in a diversity of expression, yet united in their focus on God and the Lamb. This scene describes the culmination of God's plan through history, from the division of humanity at the Tower of Babel into languages and nations (Genesis 11) and his calling of Abraham with a promise of blessing to the nations (Genesis 12), climaxing at the cross where "the wall of hostility" between Israel and the nations was broken (Ephesians 2:11–22), and then the spreading of the gospel globally through the church.

NO SOLITARY CHRISTIANS

When people come to faith in Christ, what is it that should follow? Although there are situations in which Christians are forced into isolation, the clear norm of Scripture is for believers in Christ to find fellowship with each other. Countering the esteem he once held for the solitary mystics and the error of thinking that theirs was the way to true holiness, John Wesley wrote nearly three hundred years ago: "Directly opposite to [the mystics' solitary approach to justification] is the Gospel of Christ. Solitary religion is not to be found there. 'Holy solitaries' is a phrase no more consistent with the Gospel than holy adulterers. The Gospel of Christ knows of no religion, but social; no holiness, but social holiness."[1]

If the church is to be social, not solitary, what is it to look like?

DISTORTED IMAGES OF THE CHURCH

Sadly, Christian history is full of distortions of the social nature of the church. Race in the southern United States and South Africa, caste in India, tribalism in West Africa, and even religious affiliation *before* turning to Christ have all been sinful barriers telling "other folks" that "This is *our* church; you go somewhere else." I do not need to take the time to argue that such exclusivism has its origins outside the Bible and far from the guidance of the Holy Spirit.

In a previous chapter, I mentioned the well-known Homogenous Unit Principle. The principle describes (with the limitations I noted) what happens where I lived while writing this book: most national evangelical Christians go to a church that holds services in Greek, Iranians generally attend a Farsi language service, Filipina housemaids tend to go to a service conducted in Tagalog, while Sri Lankans go to a meeting where Sinhala is spoken. All of these congregations have worship styles that fit into their cultural style and values. And the rest of us expatriates? We tend to go to one of a handful of international, English-language congregations.

It is the natural thing to do. Although I have preached for the Filipinas, my family would not have flourished in a church where most of the service is in a language we did not understand. And although most of the Greek-language churches provide translation, that adds an awkwardness that motivates us, and others like us, to become part of the easier English-language setting we enjoy.

The danger is when the *natural* thing becomes the *wrong* thing. At what point does homogeneity become exclusivism? When does the desire to have a service in a style we enjoy become a barrier to fellowship with people of another economic class, language, or age group?

At the other extreme is an unrealistic emphasis on unity that ignores reality. Ideally, Indian followers of Christ, of Dalit and Brahmin background, should sit together at the Lord's Table as well as the kitchen table; Palestinian Christians and Messianic Jews should worship God together; Turkish and Greek Cypriots who know Jesus as Lord should enjoy fellowship. We hear encouraging reports of these things beginning to happen; but while the Holy Spirit provides the spiritual power to change, it takes time to build trust and break down ancient barriers.

Superficial unity can be a mask for an imposed culture. "Sure, folks like that are welcome at our church . . . provided they do things *our* way." The final phrase may not be said aloud, but it is too often communicated. I have seen it repeatedly in international churches and gatherings, where lip service is given to diversity but one or two nationalities dominate in numbers or among the leadership.

Visiting Ghana on board OM's ship *Logos II* in 1991, together with an African leader of the Ghana Evangelism Commission, we challenged the pastors to look at the minorities among them. My colleague, from the Kasena tribe of the north of the country, had too often observed and personally been subjected to exclusive treatment in the churches, predominantly made up of majority Christian southern tribes.

The pastoral team of one church asked us what they could do. They thought that the minority Fra Fra people among them, economic immigrants from the north, simply had no interest in Christ or their church. A significant evangelistic breakthrough was made when the church backed away from the imposed unity of language (English and Fanti) and dress style (most of the Fra Fra were poor) and discovered this people's felt needs. The English classes and new worship services translated into the northern tribal language were immediately well attended and many turned to Christ.

DEMONSTRATING OUR UNITY IN CHRIST

Even among friends, our unity in Christ can be challenged by world events. When the Argentine armed forces invaded the South Atlantic islands in 1982, I was serving on board OM's ship *Doulos*. In our crew were probably fifteen Argentineans and three or four times that many British citizens. Before the invasion I would guess that most British citizens rarely thought of those distant spots of land. For Argentineans (yes, Christians included) they were a sore that had festered in the national pride for 150 years. To complicate matters, among my crewmates were some from both nations who had friends or cousins serving in the ensuing war.

Relationships were tested—but unity was maintained. Central was a daily prayer meeting exclusively for the

Argentines and British; people from other countries were not invited. Somehow they found a way to value their homelands while recognizing their common citizenship in the eternal kingdom of God.

In Christ, the barriers have been broken down; as we come to the cross, national origin, gender, and economic class offer no priority (Galatians 3:28; Colossians 3:11). Dealing with the relationship between Jewish and Gentile followers of Jesus, Paul declares that although we Gentiles once were "separate," "excluded," and "foreigners . . . without hope and without God in the world," now we "have been brought near through the blood of Christ." Among those who are "in Christ Jesus," none are "foreigners and aliens," but rather are "fellow citizens with God's people and members of God's household" (Ephesians 2:12–13, 19).

AN ONGOING TRANSFORMATION

While some things change instantly by the Holy Spirit's power, there is also an ongoing transformation of our minds, a change from being conformed to the world (Romans 12:2) to transformation into the likeness of Christ (2 Corinthians 3:18). Justification, being set right with God, takes place in a moment, but the reordering of our worldview is an ongoing process. As this transformation reaches its goal, although I may still prefer Big Macs and baseball to other foods and entertainment, at the deepest level of my being I will be more like an Amazon tribesman or Beijing businessman who shares faith in Christ than like my non-Christian fellow citizen who lives down the street.

Demonstration of this change will be worked out over time in individual lives and in the church as a whole. The Indian church, which failed in its nineteenth- and twentieth-century response to welcome Dalits as equal partners, is making steps toward embracing them as equals at the start of the twenty-first century. The change visible at the macro level, the visible acts of the church as a whole, is the composite of the change that has taken place in individual leaders, laypeople, and churches across the country.

Such change is taking place in numerous communities around the world, and was highlighted in the findings of the World Inquiry presented at the 2004 Forum for World Evangelization, sponsored by the Lausanne Committee for World Evangelization, as the key emerging mission paradigm early in the twenty-first century.[2] A search on the World Wide Web for key terms such as *transformation, reconciliation*, or *Christian* and the name of one or two well-known Christian agencies involved in community development and relief will quickly point to numerous other examples from New Zealand to South Africa to the Balkans and beyond.

How deep has transformation taken hold in you and in me? Are we truly "one people"? Or do we cling to our old ethnicity, a concept sometimes defined by the question, "Whom will you allow your daughter to marry?" In some settings today, Muslim young men who have turned to Christ are trusted—but not enough to be allowed to marry into a family of Christian origin. Even among people of apparently shared cultural values there can be differences over this issue. While I was serving as personnel director on the *Doulos* in the 1980s, the Argentine father of a young woman joining our staff exhorted me, "Don't you dare let her fall in love with a Venezuelan!" (as if I could do much to control her emotions).

There are complicated social factors involved in this issue, as well as the personal compatibility vital to any successful marriage; I do not intend to minimize their gravity. But perhaps our attitude toward marriage—in particular, marriage of our children—may help us measure just how universal we have become in our love and acceptance, our transformation across ethnic lines within the body of Christ.

"SHE WAS ONE OF US"

Lebanon is known for diversity. Over the centuries the deep valleys of its geography have helped to reinforce the divisions along the fault line of religion. Among the cultural mix in the mountains surrounding Beirut live the Druze, a people whose faith is shrouded in secrecy.

The number of Druze who have found faith in Christ has recently grown from a handful to several dozen. They find it hard to fit in among the churches of those whose cultural background is Christian. Nor, as one informed observer put it (tongue slightly in cheek), are they "Druze for Jesus." Out of step with their own ethnic group, they are somehow a "third way" of living as Christians in their country.

In November 2002 a young American nurse was murdered in the city of Sidon. An evangelical Christian, she served Muslim Palestinian women and their young children. Her death shocked the nation. A large congregation gathered for her funeral service in Beirut; among them were several

Druze men. Followers of Jesus, they had rarely set foot inside an evangelical church building before. The nurse's homeland was half a world away from theirs. Her American culture had values far different from the traditions of Lebanon's Chouf Mountains. But they came and sat and mourned.

Moved by their presence, a Western friend of the nurse and the young men asked why they had come.

"She was one of us," was their simple reply.

A NEW PEOPLE, A HOLY NATION, AND THE PURPOSE OF THE JOURNEY

I am writing these final words while away from home. Soon I will fly overnight through several time zones, crossing high over several countries of Asia and the Middle East. My wife will meet me at the airport, ready to drive me on the last hour of my journey back to our house along the southern coast of Cyprus.

Although on previous trips I have never noticed a sign referring to the city limits of our municipality, another notice on the edge of town *has* caught my eye: a sign declaring the *telos* of the multilane, high-speed highway. In modern Greek, *telos* simply means "the end." The centuries have rubbed a rich meaning off the word, something of significance as I contemplate my trip. In the New Testament, *telos* can also refer to "purpose."

When we approach that sign tomorrow, my wife will read it and recognize that the highway is coming to an *end* and will drive more slowly. Sitting in the passenger seat, I will think of the old meaning: *purpose*. The highway was built for a reason. Jet-lagged and tired though I will be, when I see that sign I will smile; I will have reached the goal, the journey will have brought me home.

You and I, like the nurse and the Druze of the previous story, may come from very different backgrounds. But as we follow Jesus, who is the only way, and find salvation through his unique cross, God transforms us. Our journeys may differ, but they have a shared *telos*—the purpose that God has in mind for his people.

Change takes place, sometimes slowly and often with cost, as God gives us a new heart and renews us at the deepest levels of our being and worldview. As we challenge the values imbibed from our cultures and allow the Holy Spirit to transform us at the core, we take on the values of this new, holy nation.

> You are a chosen people, a royal priesthood, a holy nation, a people belonging to God, that you may declare the praises of him who called you out of darkness into his wonderful light. Once you were not a people, but now you are the people of God; once you had not received mercy, but now you have received mercy. (1 Peter 2:9–10)

Becoming this God-praising people, not just saved souls in isolation, I believe is central to the goal of conversion and the purpose of God as we come to, and grow in, faith in Jesus Christ.

POSTSCRIPT

How God works in conversion presents theological and missiological questions that have intrigued me for many years. Despite much reading and observation, including serious research projects of an academic nature, I am still only beginning to probe the depths of grace and the sometimes surprising methods God employs to draw us to himself. As I listen to stories of how people have come to faith in Christ, over and over I hear the refrain of God's amazing kindness and mercy.

My purpose in writing this book has been to introduce themes that have developed in my reflection on this great topic. I hope that it has stimulated your own thinking and reflection. You have probably agreed with many of my points; at times you may have disagreed or just not understood what I meant.

If you share with me in faith in Jesus Christ as Savior and obedience to him as Lord, I am not overly concerned about disagreement on details. Let us together continue to reflect on the Word of God as it explains our human experience of conversion, aiming for "unity in the faith and in the knowledge of the Son of God" (Ephesians 4:13). If I have prompted you to deeper reflection along these themes, then my purpose in writing has been fulfilled.

Perhaps you do not share the faith in Jesus Christ that I have pointed to throughout this book. If that is the case, then in closing I invite you to consider and make your own the trustworthy saying Paul affirmed to his colleague Titus:

> When the kindness and love of God our Savior appeared, he saved us, not because of righteous things we had done, but because of his mercy. He saved us through the washing of rebirth and renewal by the Holy Spirit, whom he poured out on us generously through Jesus Christ our Savior, so that, having been justified by his grace, we might become heirs having the hope of eternal life. (Titus 3:4–7)

BIBLIOGRAPHY

Abbott, Edwin A. *Flatland: A Romance of Many Dimensions*. 6th ed., rev. New York: Dover Publications, 1952.

Ambedkar, B. R. "Why Dr. Ambedkar Renounced Hinduism." January 12, 2001. http://www.ambedkar.org/Babasaheb/Why.htm.

Barker, Kenneth L. and John R Kohlenberger III, eds. *Zondervan NIV Bible Commentary*. Pradis CD-ROM: version 5.1.50. Grand Rapids: Zondervan, 1994: Acts 8:9.

Barrett, David, and Todd M. Johnson. *World Christian Trends*. Pasadena, CA: William Carey Library, 2001.

Bono, "Bono's Remarks to the National Prayer Breakfast," Feb. 2, 2006. http://www.data.org/archives/000774.php (ellipses in the original).

Bosch, David. "The Structure of Missions: An Exposition of Matthew 28:16–20." In *Exploring Church Growth*, edited by Wilbert Shenk, 218–48. Grand Rapids: Eerdmans, 1983.

Britt, David T. "From Homogeneity to Congruence: A Church-Community Model." *Urban Mission* 8, no. 3 (January 1991): 27–41.

Bush, Luis, ed. *A Unifying Vision of the Church's Mission*. 2004 Forum for World Evangelization, Thailand, 2004.

Claerbaut, David. *Urban Ministry in a New Millennium*. Updated ed. Waynesboro, GA: Authentic, 2005.

Cleary, Edward L. "Shopping Around: Questions about Latin American Conversions." *International Bulletin of Missionary Research* 28, no. 2 (April 2004): 50–54.

D'souza, Joseph. *Dalit Freedom Now and Forever: The Epic Struggle for Dalit Emancipation*. Centennial, CO: Dalit Freedom Network; Secunderabad, India: OM Books, 2004.

Engel, James F., and H. Wilbert Norton. *What's Gone Wrong with the Harvest?* Grand Rapids: Zondervan, 1975.

Fernando, Ajith. "Some Thoughts on Missionary Burnout," *Evangelical Missions Quarterly* 35, no. 4 (October 1999): 440–43.

Garrison, David. *Church Planting Movements: How God Is Redeeming a Lost World*. Midlothian, VA: WIGTake Resources, 2004.

Glasser, Arthur. *Announcing the Kingdom*. Grand Rapids: Baker, 2003.

Gray, Frank. "The Gray Matrix," http://integralgc.com/tgm/index2.htm.

Greenlee, David H. "Christian Conversion from Islam: Social, Cultural, Communication, and Supernatural Factors in the Process of Conversion and Faithful Church Participation." PhD diss., Trinity International University, Deerfield, IL, 1996.

———. *The Heart of Missions: Poetic Reflections of God's Global Servants*. Salem, OH: Schmul, 2004.

Greenlee, David H., ed. *From the Straight Path to the Narrow Way: Journeys of Faith*. Waynesboro, GA: Authentic, 2006.

Grunlan, Stephen A., and Marvin K. Mayers. *Cultural Anthropology: A Christian Perspective*. 2nd ed. Grand Rapids: Zondervan Academie, 1988.

Habib, Gabriel. "Response to David A. Kerr." *International Bulletin of Missionary Research* 20, no. 1 (January 1996): 22.

Hampden-Turner, Charles, and Fons Trompenaars. *Building Cross-cultural Competence: How to Create Wealth from Conflicting Values*. New York: Wiley, 2000.

Hefner, Robert W., ed. *Conversion to Christianity: Historical and Anthropological Perspectives on a Great Transformation*. Berkeley and Los Angeles: University of California Press, 1993.

Hendricks, William D. *Exit Interviews: Revealing Stories of Why People Are Leaving the Church.* Chicago: Moody, 1993.

Hiebert, Paul. *Anthropological Insights for Missionaries.* Grand Rapids: Baker, 1985.

———. *Anthropological Reflections on Missiological Issues.* Grand Rapids: Baker, 1994.

———. *Cultural Anthropology.* Grand Rapids: Baker, 1983.

Howell, Richard, ed. *Transformation in Action.* 2004 Forum for World Evangelization, Thailand, 2004.

Ivereigh, Austen. "Europe of the Heart," *The Tablet,* (May 15, 2004), http://www.thetablet.co.uk/cgi-bin/register.cgi/tablet-00894.

Jansen, Gabriël. "Reaching Moroccans in Amsterdam (the Netherlands) with the Gospel." MA thesis, Tyndale Theological Seminary, Bad Hoevedorp, the Netherlands, 2000, 130.

Jayakumar, Samuel. *Dalit Consciousness and Christian Conversion: Historical Resources for a Contemporary Debate.* Delhi: ISPCK; Oxford: Regnum, 1999.

Kerr, David A. "Mission and Proselytism: A Middle Eastern Perspective." *International Bulletin of Missionary Research* 20, no. 1 (January 1996): 12–22.

Kilgour, David. "Politics and Faith in Africa: Excerpts of a Talk to Members of the Congregation of St. Bartholomew's Anglican Church, New Edinburgh, Ottawa," February 25, 2001. http://www.david-kilgour.com/faith/africafaith.htm.

Kim, John. "Muslim Villagers Coming to Faith in Christ: A Case Study and Model of Group Dynamics." In *From the Straight Path to the Narrow Way: Journeys of Faith*, edited by David Greenlee. Waynesboro, GA: Authentic, 2006.

Kim, Sebastian C. H. *In Search of Identity: Debates on Religious Conversion in India*. Oxford: Oxford University Press, 2003.

Lankaweb, "The Evils of Religious Fundamentalism Has No Place in Sri Lanka," December 28, 2003. http://www.lankaweb.com/news/editorial/281203-1.html.

Latourette, Kenneth Scott. *A History of Christianity, Volume I: Beginnings to 1500*. Rev. ed. New York: Harper and Row, 1975.

McAmis, Robert Day. *Malay Muslims: The History and Challenge of Resurgent Islam in Southeast Asia*. Grand Rapids and Cambridge: Eerdmans, 2002.

McGavran, Donald. *The Bridges of God*. New York: Friendship Press, 1955.

———. *Ethnic Realities and the Church: Lessons from India*. Pasadena, CA: William Carey Library, 1979.

———. *Understanding Church Growth*. 3rd ed. Revised and edited by C. Peter Wagner. Grand Rapids: Eerdmans, 1990.

———. "Discipling Without Dismantling the Tongue, Tribe and People." In *Mission Mandate: A Compendium on the Perspective of Missions in India*, edited by M. Ezra Sargunam, 162–79. Kilpauk, Madras, India: Mission India 2000, 1992.

Middle East Council of Churches. "Proselytism, Sects, and Pastoral Challenges: A Study Document," 1989. Quoted in David A. Kerr, 1996.

John Milton, *Paradise Lost*, Book 7, rev. 2nd ed., 1674. Available online at http://www.literature. org/authors/milton-john/paradise-lost/.

Montgomery, James, Esq. "The Missionary's Burial," *The Methodist Magazine* 7, no. 11 (November 1824): 440.

Montgomery, Robert L. "The Spread of Religions and Macrosocial Relations." *Sociological Analysis* 52, no. 1 (Spring 1991): 37–53.

Murphy, Ed. *Spiritual Warfare*. Colorado Springs: OC International, 1990.

Naugle, David K. *Worldview: The History of a Concept*. Grand Rapids: Eerdmans, 2002.

Neill, Stephen. *A History of Christian Missions*. Rev. ed. London: Penguin, 1987.

Olson, Bruce. *Bruchko*. Carol Stream, IL.: Creation House, 1978.

Padilla, C. René. "The Unity of the Church and the Homogeneous Unit Principle." *International Bulletin of Missionary Research* 6, no. 1 (January 1982): 23–30.

———. *Transforming Church and Mission*. 2004 Forum for World Evangelization, Thailand.

Peace, Richard V. *Conversion in the New Testament: Paul and the Twelve*. Grand Rapids and Cambridge: Eerdmans, 1999.

Rambo, Lewis R. *Understanding Religious Conversion*. New Haven and London: Yale University Press, 1993.

Ray, Nick. *Cambodia*, 4th ed. Melbourne, London, Oakland, Paris: Lonely Planet Guidebooks, 2002.

Robeck, Cecil M. Jr. "Mission and the Issue of Proselytism." *International Bulletin of Missionary Research* 20, no. 1 (January 1996): 2–7.

Sabra, George. "Orthodox-Evangelical Dialogue: An MECC Perspective." *MECC News Report* 10 (1998): 2–3.

Samuel, Vinay and Chris Sugden, eds. *Mission as Transformation: A Theology of the Whole Gospel*, (Oxford: Regnum Books, 1999), 263–64.

Sargunam, M. Ezra. "People Groups and People Movements." In *Mission Mandate: A Compendium on the Perspective of Missions in India*, edited by M. Ezra Sargunam. Kilpauk, Madras, India: Mission India 2000, 1992: 180–91.

Singh, Manpreet. "Anti-Conversion Conspiracy." *Christianity Today* (May 2004). http://www.christianitytoday.com/ct/2004/005/13.20.html.

Smith, Donald. *Creating Understanding*. Grand Rapids: Zondervan, 1992.

Søgaard, Viggo. *Media in Church and Mission: Communicating the Gospel.* Pasadena, CA: William Carey Library, 1993.

Suleiman, Michael W. "Morocco in the Arab and Muslim World: Attitudes of Moroccan Youth." *The Maghreb Review.* Vol. 14, no. 1–2 (1989):16–27.

Swan, William. "The Converted Heathen." *The Methodist Magazine.* Vol. 11, no. 7 (July 1828): 280.

Tertullian. *Apology.* Chaps. XXII, XXX, and XXXII. Translated by S. Thelwall. http://www.ccel. org/fathers2/ANF-03/anf03-05.htm#P253_53158.

Van Engen, Chuck. "Toward a Missiology of Transformation." In *A Unifying Vision of the Church's Mission*, edited by Luis Bush (2004): 93–117.

Wagner, C. Peter. *Our Kind of People: The Ethical Dimensions of Church Growth in America.* Atlanta: J. Knox Press, 1979.

Walls, Andrew F. "Converts or Proselytes? The Crisis over Conversion in the Early Church." *International Bulletin of Missionary Research* 28, no. 1 (January 2004): 2–6.

Warraq, Ibn, ed. *Leaving Islam: Apostates Speak Out.* Amherst, NY: Prometheus, 1993.

Wells, David. *God in the Wasteland.* Grand Rapids: Eerdmans; Leicester, England: Inter-Varsity, 1994.

Wesley, John. Preface to *Hymns and Sacred Poems*, by John Wesley and Charles Wesley. London: William Strahan, 1739.

————. *The Journal of the Rev. John Wesley*, A.M. edited by Nehemiah Cornock. London: Charles H. Kelley. ca. 1909.

Wheaton Consultation. "Transformation: The Church in Response to Human Need." In *Mission as Transformation: A Theology of the Whole Gospel*, edited by Vinay Samuel and Chris Sugden, 261–76. Oxford: Regnum Books, 1999. http://www.ad2000.org/re00620.htm.

Wiher, Hannes. *Shame and Guilt: A Key to Cross-Cultural Ministry*. Edition IWG, Mission Academics, Band 10. Bonn, Germany: Verlag für Kultur und Wissenschaft, 2003.

World Evangelical Alliance. 2003. "Definition of Proselytism and Evangelism," October, 2003. http://www.worldevangelicals.org/news/news_proselytism_28oct03.htm.

NOTES

Chapter 1

1   Richard V. Peace, *Conversion in the New Testament: Paul and the Twelve* (Grand Rapids and Cambridge: Eerdmans, 1999).

2   Ibid., 286.

3   Andrew F. Walls, "Converts or Proselytes? The Crisis over Conversion in the Early Church," *International Bulletin of Missionary Research* 28, no. 1 (January 2004): 2–6.

Chapter 2

1   Paul Hiebert, "The Category *Christian* in the Mission Task," in *Anthropological Reflections on Missiological Issues* (Grand Rapids: Baker, 1994), 107–39.

2   William D. Hendricks, *Exit Interviews: Revealing Stories of Why People Are Leaving the Church* (Chicago: Moody, 1993), 266–67.

3   Nehemiah Curnock, ed., *The Journal of the Rev. John Wesley, A.M.,* vol. 5, entry for August 25, 1763 (London: Charles H. Kelly, ca. 1909), 26.

Chapter 3

1   James F. Engel and H. Wilbert Norton, *What's Gone Wrong with the Harvest?* (Grand Rapids: Zondervan, 1975), available online at http://www.newwway.org/engel/. See also "An Interpersonal Communication Model: The Engel Scale Explained" at http://guide.gospelcom.net/resources/telli-toften.php.

2   Viggo Søgaard, *Media in Church and Mission: Communicating the Gospel* (Pasadena, CA: William Carey Library, 1993).

3   Jim Engel has assured me that the scale was never intended to reflect a purely cognitive understanding of the gospel. David Barrett and Todd Johnson, *World Christian Trends* (Pasadena, CA: William Carey Library, 2001), 745, although too critical of the Engel Scale's practical usefulness, point out that in practice its use has focused on "an intellectual grasp of Christian truths."

4   Paul Hiebert, "Worldview Transformation," in *From the Straight Path to the Narrow Way: Journeys of Faith*, ed. David Greenlee (Waynesboro, GA: Authentic, 2006), 26.

5   David Greenlee, "Christian Conversion from Islam:
Social, Cultural, Communication, and Supernatural
Factors in the Process of Conversion and Faithful Church
Participation" (PhD diss., Trinity International University,
1996), 67–70.

6   Michael W. Suleiman, "Morocco in the Arab and Muslim
World: Attitudes of Moroccan Youth," *The Maghreb Review*,
Vol. 14, no. 1–2 (1989): 16–27.

7   Donald Smith, *Creating Understanding* (Grand Rapids:
Zondervan, 1992), 142–43.

8   David Wells, *God in the Wasteland* (Grand Rapids:
Eerdmans; Leicester, England: Inter-Varsity, 1994), 180–81.

9   Frank Gray, "The Gray Matrix," available online at
http://integralgc.com/tgm/index2.htm. This website includes
a number of useful illustrations and applications of this
model.

10   Ajith Fernando, "Some Thoughts on Missionary
Burnout," *Evangelical Missions Quarterly* 35, no. 4
(October 1999): 440–43.

11   After writing this chapter I read David K. Naugle's
book, *Worldview: The History of a Concept* (Grand Rapids:
Eerdmans, 2002). Chapter 9, "Theological Reflections on
'Worldview,'" gives a very helpful discussion of the relationship of the heart, as described in the Bible, and worldview.

Chapter 4

1   The name of the location has been changed due to the sensitivity of the situation.

2   Taken from John Kim, "Muslim Villagers Coming to Faith in Christ: A Case Study and Model of Group Dynamics," in *From the Straight Path to the Narrow Way: Journeys of Faith*, ed. David Greenlee (Waynesboro, GA: Authentic, 2006), 239–53.

3   See, for example, Joseph D'souza, *Dalit Freedom Now and Forever: The Epic Struggle for Dalit Emancipation* (Secunderabad, India: OM Books; Centennial, CO: Dalit Freedom Network, 2004).

4   See http://www.bruceolson.com or Bruce Olson, *Bruchko* (Carol Stream, IL: Creation House, 1978), for a detailed account.

5   Kenneth Scott Latourette, *A History of Christianity, Volume I: Beginnings to 1500*, rev. ed. (New York: Harper and Row, 1975), 350.

6   Stephen Neill, *A History of Christian Missions*, rev. ed. (London: Penguin, 1987), 66.

7   Austen Ivereigh, "Europe of the Heart," *The Tablet*, May 15, 2004, http://www.thetablet.co.uk/cgi-bin/register.cgi/tablet-00894. See also http://www.miteinander-wie-sonst.de/, the official website of the event.

8   Donald McGavran, *Understanding Church Growth*, 3rd ed., revised and edited by C. Peter Wagner (Grand Rapids: Eerdmans, 1990), 225.

9   David Garrison, *Church Planting Movements: How God Is Redeeming a Lost World* (Midlothian, VA: WIGTake Resources, 2004), 21. Also available online in an earlier version at http://www.imb.org/CPM.

10 Ibid., 221.

11 Ibid., 228.

12 This is described in various chapters in Greenlee, *From the Straight Path*.

13 Charles Hampden-Turner and Fons Trompenaars, *Building Cross-Cultural Competence: How to Create Wealth from Conflicting Values* (New York: Wiley, 2000), 71–72.

14 This is not the same country referred to earlier where I had done research among young men who had come to faith.

Chapter 5

1   Donald McGavran, *Understanding Church Growth*, 3rd ed., revised and edited by C. Peter Wagner (Grand Rapids: Eerdmans, 1990), 163.

2   Donald McGavran, *The Bridges of God* (New York: Friendship Press, 1955).

3   Donald McGavran, *Ethnic Realities and the Church: Lessons from India* (Pasadena, CA: William Carey Library, 1979), 82.

4   McGavran, *Understanding Church Growth*, 225.

5   McGavran, *Bridges of God*, 49, 55–57.

6   McGavran, *Ethnic Realities*, 95.

7   C. Peter Wagner, *Our Kind of People: The Ethical Dimensions of Church Growth in America* (Atlanta: J. Knox Press, 1979), 9, 30.

8   Ibid., 133, 136.

9   Ibid., 77, 103.

10 C. René Padilla, "The Unity of the Church and the Homogeneous Unit Principle," *International Bulletin of Missionary Research* 6, no. 1 (January 1982), 23–30.

11 David Bosch, "The Structure of Missions: An Exposition of Matthew 28:16–20," in *Exploring Church Growth*, ed. Wilbert Shenk (Grand Rapids: Eerdmans, 1983), 218–48.

12 M. Ezra Sargunam, "People Groups and People Movements," in *Mission Mandate: A Compendium on the Perspective of Missions in India*, ed. M. Ezra Sargunam (Kilpauk, Madras, India: Mission India 2000, 1992), 180–91.

13 David T. Britt, "From Homogeneity to Congruence: A Church-Community Model," *Urban Mission* 8, no. 3 (January 1991): 27–41.

14 Charles Hampden-Turner and Fons Trompenaars, *Building Cross-Cultural Competence: How to Create Wealth from Conflicting Values* (New York: Wiley, 2000), 189–233.

15 David Claerbaut, *Urban Ministry in a New Millennium*, updated edition (Waynesboro, GA: Authentic, 2005), 205–32.

16 Gabriël Jansen, "Reaching Moroccans in Amsterdam (the Netherlands) with the Gospel" (MA thesis, Tyndale Theological Seminary, Bad Hoevedorp, the Netherlands, 2000), 130.

17 Hannes Wiher, *Shame and Guilt: A Key to Cross-Cultural Ministry* (Bonn, Germany: Edition IWG, Mission Academics, Band 10, Verlag für Kultur und Wissenschaft, 2003), 367. Wiher refers to Robert Priest, "Missionary Elenctics: Conscience and Culture," *Missiology* 22, no. 3 (July 1994): 291–315.

Chapter 6

1 Bono, "Bono's Remarks to the National Prayer Breakfast," Feb. 2, 2006. http://www.data.org/archives/000774.php (ellipses in the original).

2 I base this on the understanding that Peter was the source of much of Mark's information. Note, for example, the progression of events following the first mass feeding on the Jewish side of the Sea of Galilee (Mark 6:30–44). Concluding the story of Jesus walking on the water, Mark notes that the disciples were amazed because "they did not understand about the loaves" and that "their hearts were

hardened" (Mark 6:52). After landing at Gennesaret, not
the intended destination of Bethsaida (Mark 6:45, 53), Jesus
dealt with the issue of "clean and unclean" (Mark 7:1–23),
including a challenge to the disciples, in a style normally
reserved for the Pharisees, "Are you so dull?" (Mark
7:18). Significantly, this is followed by the story of the
Syrophoenician woman who received some of the "crumbs,"
the welcome of Jesus to the Gentile Decapolis, and the second mass feeding "during those days" (Mark 7:24–8:10).
Shortly after this, Jesus spoke to the disciples about the symbolism in the total number of loaves he had multiplied, and
the amount gathered afterward, in the two mass feedings on
the Jewish and then on the Gentile side of the Sea of Galilee,
asking, "Do you still not understand?" (Mark 8:17–21).
Arriving in Bethsaida, the unreached destination following the first mass feeding and the hometown of Peter (John
1:44), Jesus healed a blind man in two steps (Mark 8:22–26).
I believe that Mark (and Peter) told the story in this way to
illustrate Peter's own process of overcoming spiritual blind-
ness and finally understanding about the "bread" available
to both Jews and Gentiles. It is very significant that immediately following this healing Mark records Peter's confession
that Jesus was the Christ (Mark 8:27–30).

3   Editorial, *Mission Frontiers* 27, no. 5 (September–
October 2005): 4.

4   Frank Decker, "When 'Christian' Does Not Translate,"
Good News Magazine, May–June 2005, http://www.good-
newsmag.org/magazine/3MayJune/MJ05msum.htm (italics
in the original).

5   John and Anna Travis, "Contextualization among Muslims, Hindus, and Buddhists: A Focus on 'Insider Movements,'" *Mission Frontiers* 27, no. 5 (September–October 2005): 12. This helpful article is available in the archives section of http://www.missionfrontiers.org. Other helpful articles can be found in the archives of the *International Journal of Foreign Missions* at http://www.ijfm.org.

6   Herbert Hoefer, *Churchless Christianity* (Pasadena, CA: William Carey Library, 2001), xv.

7   Ibid., 58–59 (italics in the original).

8   For a detailed discussion of the issues involved here, see Harold A. Netland, *Dissonant Voices: Religious Pluralism and the Question of Truth* (Grand Rapids: Eerdmans, 1991).

9   *Mission Frontiers* 27, no. 5 (September–October 2005).

Chapter 7

1   Arthur Glasser, *Announcing the Kingdom* (Grand Rapids: Baker, 2003), 156.

2   David A. Kerr, "Mission and Proselytism: A Middle East Perspective," *International Bulletin of Missionary Research* 20, no. 1 (1996): 12–22; and Gabriel Habib, "Response to David A. Kerr," *International Bulletin of Missionary Research* 20, no. 1 (1996): 22.

3   Cecil M. Robeck Jr., "Mission and the Issue of Proselytism," *International Bulletin of Missionary Research* 20, no. 1 (1996): 2–7.

4   George Sabra, "Orthodox-Evangelical Dialogue: An MECC Perspective," *MECC News Report* 10, no. 2–3 (1998).

5   Nick Ray, *Cambodia*, 4th ed. (Melbourne, London, Oakland, Paris: Lonely Planet Guidebooks, 2002), 52.

6   Editorial, "The Evils of Religious Fundamentalism Has No Place in Sri Lanka," *Lankaweb*, December 28, 2003, http://www.lankaweb.com/news/editorial/281203-1.html.

7   Manpreet Singh, "Anti-Conversion Conspiracy," *Christianity Today*, May 2004, http://www.christianitytoday. com/ct/2004/005/13.20.html.

8   World Evangelical Alliance, "Definition of Proselytism and Evangelism," October, 2003, http://www.worldevangeli- cals.org/news/news_proselytism_28oct03.htm.

9   Glasser, *Announcing the Kingdom,* 351.

Chapter 8

1   John Milton, *Paradise Lost*, Book 7, rev. 2nd ed., (1674), available online at http://www.literature. org/authors/milton-john/paradise-lost/.

2   Edwin A. Abbott, *Flatland: A Romance of Many Dimensions*, 6th ed., rev. (New York: Dover Publications, 1952).

3   David Greenlee and Rick Love, "Conversion through the Looking Glass," in *From the Straight Path to the Narrow Way: Journeys of Faith*, ed. David Greenlee (Waynesboro, GA: Authentic, 2006), 37.

4   Two books on the topic of the social implications of conversion that I have found helpful are Lewis R. Rambo, *Understanding Religious Conversion* (New Haven and London: Yale University Press, 1993), and Robert W. Hefner, ed., *Conversion to Christianity: Historical and Anthropological Perspectives on a Great Transformation* (Berkeley and Los Angeles: University of California Press, 1993).

5   Ibn Warraq, ed., *Leaving Islam: Apostates Speak Out* (Amherst, NY: Prometheus, 1993), 92.

6   Ali Sina, "Why I Left Islam," in Ibn Warraq, *Apostates Speak Out*, 156.

7   See references to McGavran and Garrison in chapter 4.

8   Samples of the *Firm Foundations* series are available online at http://www.ntm.org/books/ffless.html.

9   William D. Hendricks, *Exit Interviews: Revealing Stories of Why People Are Leaving the Church* (Chicago: Moody, 1993), 11.

Chapter 9

1   James Montgomery, Esq., "The Missionary's Burial," *The Methodist Magazine* 7, no. 11, November 1824, 440.

The entire poem is reproduced in David Greenlee, *The Heart of Missions: Poetic Reflections of God's Global Servants* (Salem, OH: Schmul, 2004), 73–74 .

2   Paul Hiebert, *Cultural Anthropology*, 2nd ed. (Grand Rapids: Baker, 1983), 336.

3   Stephen A. Grunlan and Marvin K. Mayers, *Cultural Anthropology: A Christian Perspective*, 2nd ed. (Grand Rapids: Zondervan Academie Books, 1988), 202–3.

4   David Kilgour's website, "Politics and Faith in Africa: Excerpts of a Talk to Members of the Congregation of St. Bartholomew's Anglican Church, New Edinburgh, Ottawa," February 25, 2001, http://www.david-kilgour.com/faith/africafaith.htm. For further information see Cédric Mayrargue, "The Politics of New Religious Movements in Benin Republic: Christian Churches, Democratic Consolidation and Political Parties," April 2001, http://www.essex.ac.uk/ECPR/events/jointsessions/paperarchive/grenoble/ws13/mayrargue.pdf.

5   Robert L. Montgomery, "The Spread of Religions and Macrosocial Relations," *Sociological Analysis* 52, no. 1 (Spring 1991): 37–53.

6   Sebastian C. H. Kim, *In Search of Identity: Debates on Religious Conversion in India* (New Delhi: Oxford University Press, 2003), 66–72.

7   Montgomery, "Spread of Religions," 50.

8   B. R. Ambedkar's website, "Why Dr. Ambedkar Renounced Hinduism," January 12, 2001, http://www. ambedkar.org/Babasaheb/Why.htm.

9   Numerous publications on the World Wide Web (such as http://www.dalitnetwork.org), as well as books such as Joseph D'souza's *Dalit Freedom: Now and Forever* (Secunderabad, India: OM Books; Centennial, CO: Dalit Freedom Network, 2004), lend useful insights into this complex movement. For a historical review, including a response to Dalit liberation theologians, see Samuel Jayakumar, *Dalit Consciousness and Christian Conversion: Historical Resources for a Contemporary Debate* (Delhi: ISPCK; Oxford: Regnum, 1999).

10 Jayakumar, *Dalit Consciousness*, 357–58.

11 For example, see articles at http://www.opendoorsuk.org/ article_heroes05.php and http://www.cswusa.com/Countries/ Mexico.htm.

12 Tertullian, *Apology*, Chapters XXX and XXXII, trans. S. Thelwall, available online at http://www.ccel. org/fathers2/ANF-03/anf03-05.htm#P384_181134.

13 The consultation's final statement is posted on various websites, including http://www.ad2000.org/re00620.htm.

14 See the EFI statement at http://www.imaindia.org/press/ EFI_Press.htm.

15 "Transformation: The Church in Response to Human Need," in *Mission as Transformation: A Theology of the*

Whole Gospel, ed. Vinay Samuel and Chris Sugden (Oxford: Regnum Books, 1999), 263–64.

16 Chuck Van Engen, "Toward a Missiology of Transformation," in *A Unifying Vision of the Church's Mission*, Luis Bush, ed., 2004 Forum for World Evangelization, Thailand, September 2004.

17 René Padilla, *Transforming Church and Mission*, 2004 Forum for World Evangelization, Thailand, September 2004, 1–2, 5.

18 My criticism is not of short-term ministry in general. My concern is with "ministry" that has little do with service, witness, and personal transformation and much to do with making the participants feel good about themselves at little real cost and lacking identification with those they have ostensibly gone to serve.

Chapter 10

1 See, for example, Paul G. Hiebert, "Biblical Perspectives on Spiritual Warfare," in *Anthropological Reflections on Missiological Issues* (Grand Rapids: Baker, 1994), 203–15.

2 Ed Murphy, *Spiritual Warfare* (Colorado Springs: OC International, 1990). See also Ed Murphy, *The Handbook for Spiritual Warfare*, revised and updated (Nashville: Thomas Nelson, 2003).

3 *Zondervan NIV Bible Commentary*, ed. Kenneth L. Barker and John R. Kohlenberger III, Pradis CD-ROM: Acts 8:9, version 5.1.50 (Grand Rapids: Zondervan, 1994).

4 William Swan, "The Converted Heathen," *The Methodist Magazine* 11, no. 7, July 1828, 280.

5 Tertullian, *Apology*, Chapter XXII, trans. S. Thelwall, available online at http://www.ccel. org/fathers2/ANF-03/anf03-05.htm#P353_152127.

Chapter 11

1 John Wesley, Preface to *Hymns and Sacred Poems*, by John Wesley and Charles Wesley (London: William Strahan, 1739).

2 See for example Luis Bush, ed., *A Unifying Vision of the Church's Mission*, and Richard Howell, ed., *Transformation in Action*, published by the Lausanne Committee for that event, and the Forum's Lausanne Occasional Papers, available online at http://www.lausanne.org/Brix?pageID=13890.

Raised by missionary parents in South America, David Greenlee has served with Operation Mobilization since 1977. Having met on OM's ship *Logos*, he and his Swiss wife, Vreni, have three children, born in Germany, the United States, and the Ivory Coast. David currently serves as OM's International Research Associate. His ministry has included service on OM's ships *Logos*, *Logos II*, and *Doulos*, teaching in seminaries and Bible colleges in Europe and Asia, and research to aid mission leaders to gain further insights into how God is working in the world today. David received a PhD in Intercultural Studies from Trinity Evangelical Divinity School, Deerfield, Illinois. He is the author of *The Heart of Missions: Poetic Reflections of God's Global Servants* (Schmul, 2004) and the editor of *Global Passion: Marking George Verwer's Contribution to World Mission* (Authentic, 2003) and *From the Straight Path to the Narrow Way: Journeys of Faith* (Authentic, 2006).